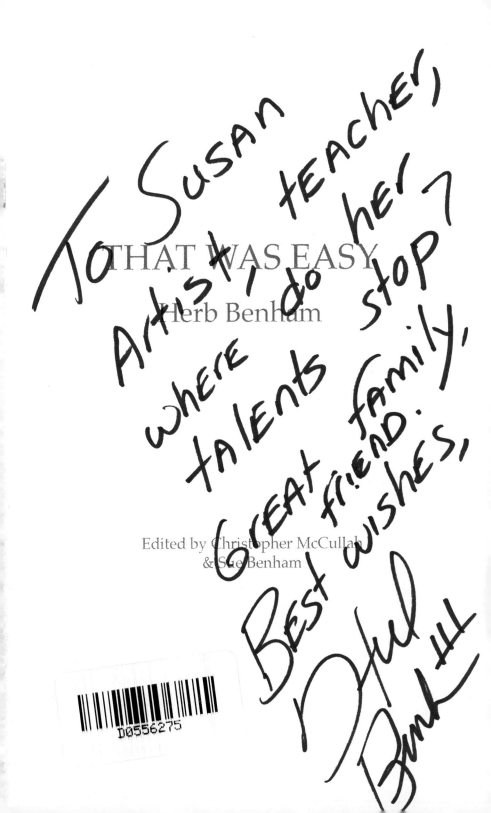

THAT WAS EASY

Herb Benham

Edited by Christopher McCullah
& Sue Benham

To Susan teacher, Artist, I do her where talents stop Great family friend. Best wishes,

Benham

© 2014, The Bakersfield Californian,
part of the TBC Media family of products

ISBN 978-0-9852407-5-2

Book design:
Glenn Hammett and Christopher McCullah

Photos courtesy of The Bakersfield Californian photographers:
Henry A. Barrios
Felix Adamo
John Harte

Special Thanks to:
The Benham Family

TABLE OF CONTENTS:

Sam and the Yo-Yo 4

Hair Turns Gray / Stones Still Roll 6

Carpool 8

Sam and Football 10

Snow 12

Quitting History Day 15

Charles Werner 17

Good Babysitter 19

After Shower 22

Biking and the Art of Saying Goodbye 24

One Last Dance 26

Pomegranates 28

Recliner 31

September and the Fair 33

Chillin' 35

Run Like the Wind 37

Dog on Roof 41

Ping Pong Pow 43

Pretty in Paris 45

Herbie's Room 49

My Rap Career 51

Selling the Caliente Suburban 53

First Job 56

Sam Leaves 58

Performance Sketchy 61

Going to Bed Mad 63

John and Bev Move to Bakersfield 65

Herbie Turns 21 68
Old Truck 70
Dad's 80th 72
Teddy 75
Hot Sauce 78
Bob Rutledge 82
The West Wing 85
Father and Son Doubles... 87
Free Jacuzzi.. 89
Goodbye Polo... 91
Collector's Corner.. 94
Sam and a Second Chance.. 97
Carrie Mae Hill.. 101
Barbershop Escape... 106
Prom Night 108
Mom's 80th 110
All Clear 113
A Smoking Deal 115
Blind Faith.. 118
Neighbors from Outer Space 121
Hitting the Pavement 123
Sue Gets Rich... 125
What's Next 127
Graduation and the Giving Tree................................ 129
Dude 131
Dominic... 133
Taking Thomas to College 137
Thanksgiving Flow 139

Is the Tree Straight? 141
Wii Win.. 143
Thomas the Vegetarian...................................... 145
Troncones and Sharks 147
Inauguration.. 150
Wake Up Dad 153
A Home for Tennis... 155
Short Stack is Not Short 157
Meeting Hunter's Parents 160
He Found His Way 162
Pot in Hondarribia.. 164
Normandy.. 167
P90X 170
Hat's Off.. 173
This One Doesn't Cry.. 176
I Say Yes.. 179
Del Mar.. 181
Wedding 184
Dad Serves Up Some Punch at the Reception 188
Wendy Wayne 191
Callie Comes Home... 196
A Proposal That Pleases All in Family.............. 200
Epilogue 203

ACKNOWLEDGEMENTS

Thank you, Bakersfield Californian, for giving me 25 years
in the playground. I've had fun.

Thanks to my editors over the years — Andy Kehe, Lois Henry,
Robert Price and especially Jennifer Self — who have saved me
from some embarrassing moments.

To Katie, Herbie, Sam and Thomas, who've shown grace and good
humor about being dragged into my columns year after year.
You've been a rich source of material. I love you.

To Sue, a great editor, friend, wife and the person
who has helped me spin many of these dreams.

FOREWORD

Herb Benham can make me believe I want to live in Bakersfield. For an LA-loving girl, that's quite some declaration. That's how good a writer he is.

Everyone thinks it's easy, being a columnist. You just sit down and begin nattering about yourself and the people you know, and when you hit 800 words, you stop writing. [This is what I call the computer ownership fallacy: just because you can type doesn't mean you can write.] And if you work and live in a town—a small city, Bakersfield, with a town-like sense of itself—there's an assumption that those 800 words should be even easier.

In fact, it's harder. Harder to write and live in a place where everybody knows you, where everyone can have a bone to pick, or his own version to tell, because odds are that the reader knows someone who lives next door to someone who went to school with the guy you wrote about in this column and he'll have a thing or two to say about what you wrote.

In our brave new online world, we've been told that the globe is our hometown, that we live in a virtual community. Herb inhabits a real community, and, in print, he reminds his readers why it matters.

Read what he had to say about a once-in-a-lifetime snowfall in a town whose summers are such scorchers that it's the place for TV reporters to test out that cliché of frying an egg on the sidewalk.

"Bakersfield is good for one of everything. A shark's skeleton on top of a dusty hill. Floods that would make the Bible proud. Monsoon rains, the Virgin Mary appearing on the side of a house, a 100-foot-high cactus, the worst possible murders imaginable, winds capable of carrying Dorothy back to Kansas. Monday's snow had them all beat. It made all the disasters and the other impressive feats of nature seem inconsequential. It covered power poles, cars, trees, and, for a moment, our sins."

Before he turns his lens to his neighbors and friends, Herb turns it on himself, sometimes disarmingly and self-deprecatingly, as in a knowing and self-knowing column full of astonishment about the disappearing contents of a gift bottle of Scotch: "Scotch travels easy. A glass goes from the table to the recliner to the bedside table as easily as a pair of reading glasses or a book of short stories."

Or this, about burying his beloved rescue dog Polo. "Every day since the day he came home with me, he would wait for me in the garage with his back against the Jacuzzi. It was an odd sort of security pillow. He would look up to me as if to say, "When are you going to hook this thing up?" I committed Polo and that ugly golden blanket to the rich, dark downtown soil. Someday, there will be a Jacuzzi next to his grave and he will be home again."

Ever hear of "habituation"? It's the phenomenon by which we get accustomed to things—sights, people, tastes. It's why the second and third bites of anything, even the most sublime food in the world, never tastes as good as the first.

I get so used to seeing the Hollywood sign that only when I'm on an airplane and all the tourists on the wrong side of the plane unbuckle their seatbelts and rush over to get a look at the thing that I realize again, yes, Hollywood is my home town. And in this state where, to use author Leo Braudy's phrase, the "frenzy of renown" is an Olympic-scale pursuit, Herb finds the storyteller's treasure in the diurnal, the modest, the untrumpeted, all right outside his front door, and sometimes inside it.

Herb's columns don't suffer from "habituation" because he doesn't. He lives in the place he writes about, but he retains a sense of wonder and novelty about it, about its comforts and its limits and its frustrations—affectionate but not sentimental, clear-eyed but not blasé.

It's a high-wire act, all right. Three times a week for 25 years, and now, here. Read them, and you'll feel like going over to his place, that hundred-year-old money pit with the leaky Jacuzzi, to borrow a cup of sugar and gab a little, for no matter where you live, this will make him your neighbor.

Patt Morrison.

L.A. Times

Patt Morrison is a utility player: newspaper, radio, television. She has a share of two Pulitzer Prizes as a writer and columnist for the Los Angeles Times. She earned six Emmys for her program hosting and commentaries work on KCET, public television in Southern California, and a half-dozen Golden Mikes as host of her talk show on KPCC, the NPR news station in Los Angeles. She is the author of the best-seller Rio LA, Tales from the Los Angeles River, and contributor to the popular mystery short story anthology, Los Angeles Noir. Pink's, the legendary Hollywood hot dog stand, named its veggie hot dog after Patt.

SAM AND THE YO-YO

Last night Sam came in and asked if I wanted a martini.

A martini? It was early for a martini, but thoughtful of him to ask. Before I could answer, he got out his yo-yo and spun it down in that flinging motion, then doubled the string into the triangular shape of a martini glass, swung the yo-yo back and forth (still in the sleeping position), let it fall to the ground and then brought it back up again.

A martini, yo-yo style.

Yo-yos are back. No matter how sophisticated we become, the fact that a wooden, plastic or metal disc can still capture the imagination of a generation of mostly boys is enough to make you want to throw your sweater over your shoulder and whistle. It is a vote for the simple, old-fashioned and low-tech.

They're hot.

A friend gave yo-yos to his staff. No more sleepy staff meetings.

Another took his son to Walmart last week. They'd called ahead. Yes, we have yo-yo's. By the time they got there, Walmart was out. They had a scene. That boy wanted a yo-yo. He had yo-yo money but no yo-yo. That was one disappointed boy.

I gave each of the kids a wooden yo-yo for Christmas. Three bucks a pop. Three bucks — that's what a toy should cost.

A package of string is another couple bucks. Good, loose string is important. With loose string, you can do tricks like the martini or the bra (think circles), two of the hottest moves in the business.

There aren't many tricks in the yo-yo world. It doesn't take years to become an expert. No need for $20-an-hour lessons. Yo-yo-ing is simple. After a week, you're in the top 10 in California. Within two weeks, Duncan is calling you for endorsements.

Making a yo-yo sleep — having it pause and sing at the bottom of its arc — is the basic move in any credible yo-yo career. That's pure sweetness. It says I am in control, I'm the guy.

If you can't do that, think about switching to jacks, Pick-Up-Stix or marbles. When you've mastered yo-yo sleep, it's time to take the dog for a walk. Then call the airlines because you're going around the world.

The yo-yo is versatile. Not only is it a good way to avoid studying, setting the table or taking out the recycling, but it's something new to fight over. You can't have too many of those things when you have kids. Somebody borrows somebody's and pretty soon they are wrestling and threatening the furniture.

A yo-yo is also an excellent tool with which to drive your mother crazy. Pretend she's lecturing you for not having done your math homework or because you forgot about a vocab test.

Look at her as if you are paying her the respect she deserves, but spin your yo-yo at the same time to relieve the stress that she is inflicting on you.

The other day, Thomas drank eight of Sam's martinis before Sam cut him off. "You've had enough," he said. "I don't want you to get drunk."

Then he was off looking for more customers. He had a couple of bras to get rid of.

HAIR TURNS GRAY /
STONES STILL ROLL

Please allow me to introduce myself.

I'm a man who's just attended a Stones concert.

My brothers treated me to a ticket to the Rolling Stones concert in Oakland on Wednesday. They bought tickets from a guy named Jimmy. Last name? Not important.

Wednesday morning, I was trying to let it loose so I could leave town, but the kids were slow in going to school. Didn't they know they shouldn't "Play with Fire?"

"Your Dad is finding out that 'You can't always get want you want,'" Sue said.

A few minutes later, the kids were still there and so my funny wife says, "It looks like your Dad can't get no 'Satisfaction.'"

What she had forgotten was that "if you try something, you just might find, you get what you need."

It rained driving up. I put good gas in the car. I usually buy the cheap stuff because I assume it's just one big tank down there under the station, but premium gas makes your car run quiet. I'm assuming people care.

In Wasco, I saw a sign that read, "Foot Scale." I've wondered how heavy feet were. Are they in the 6-pound bass range or more in the Timberlines with sand in the bottoms?

We skipped Pearl Jam, the opening act, not because they weren't good and from Seattle, the suicide capital of the world, but because we had a decision to make. Pearl Jam or dinner. Dinner won.

You know a Stones concert is starting for two reasons. First, that is the moment several people in your row choose to go to the snack bar. You just ate dinner, give it a rest.

Second, you know the Stones are close because you feel the pounding in your legs. It's like the coming of rain. Your back starts hurting well before the first drop hits the pavement.

Jagger can still sing, but he's not stupid. When you get older, and can afford it, you hire the world's best woman gospel singer, who can rattle the drink lids in the snack bar.

Now, all he has to do is hire someone to dance for him. The man can't dance, but he throws himself around with such confidence, you'd think he was leading "Soul Train." He elevates spasticity to art.

In every concert, there comes a critical moment. The one where you ask yourself, "Am I having fun?"

I'm standing up. I appear to be yelling. My brother has his arms in the air in a pose I believe he'll later regret. And when Jagger wails on "Sympathy for the Devil," it's hard not to break into a big smile.

Was I having fun? Of course I was. This was history. I was seeing the Stones. I was with my brothers and sister-in-law. None of us were going to live forever, although if Keith Richards can, our odds improve.

Still, with the smoke, the fireworks, the huge oval-shaped screen, the concert reminded me of The Wizard of Oz. The part when Dorothy and her crew discover that behind that huge face on the screen, the big booming face, is not Oz, but Mr. Oatmeal.

Pass the torch, baby. It's been a magnificent run. I couldn't get no satisfaction, but now I have.

CARPOOL

Monday is my day for carpool. I look forward to it. It's a way of spending a few unhurried minutes (unhurried, save the sprint to the car) with the kids, a time when I can listen to some 7:30-in-the-morning conversations that may include news about grandmothers's latest bipolar boyfriend.

Protocol dictates that a parent may never start a conversation in the carpool. If he or she does, that conversation will die a slow, ugly carpool death. The discussion will resemble a run-over snake. While it may wiggle, this snake will never bite anybody.

At the beginning of the year, passengers are reluctant to talk. To go to school. To do most anything but stare out the window. That changes. They get in the groove. Find a place at school. By June, riders are confident, almost bored with having prevailed over this paper tiger.

In October, one of the girls, a lively sort, came to the car with her shoes off. It was duly noted by the other passengers, one of whom said, "You just got on the board."

On the board. The big board. Whether you liken it to the giant screen at Times Square, a sign on the Jersey Turnpike or a chalkboard at school, the point is, you are busted.

Infraction begets infraction. One can get on the board for not wearing socks, for keeping the carpool waiting, or, as one of the drivers discovered, for neglecting to have your tie fully knotted.

Yet to be added to the board is eating a cinnamon roll in the car, drinking a cup of coffee or showing too much interest in a conversation unfolding in the back seat.

It is silliness — of course it is silliness — but like water in these dry parts, or money in these lean times, when can we have too much?

Tuesday through Friday, I am relieved by the gentleman whose tie was not fully knotted and thus became an entry on the board despite his efforts to articulate his way off.

On the days he drives, the carpool plays a game called Word of the Day. Consider it a warm-up for the educational possibilities of school. The driver identifies a word from his early morning newspaper reading and tosses it to the passenger as an animal trainer might throw fish to seals. In this case, passengers chew on the word and then try to decipher its meaning. Words come and go, but riders can count on collaborate and corroborate making once-a-year appearances.

Recently, one of the passengers counterattacked by springing a Word of the Day on the game's originator. This intellectual revolutionary had skipped the newspaper and gone straight to the dictionary. He stumped the stumper in a maneuver so bold that to not put him on the board would have left everybody disappointed.

Eventually the carpoolers must disembark. This is the drop-off, and rules pertain here too. One should never expect the carpoolers to exit the vehicle at any other place than directly in front of the entrance. A suggestion to the contrary is met with stares icier than Tule fog.

While the trip to school is lively, driving back home with an empty car is a good time to sort out the flurry of activity, the moving, the rushing toward some inevitable promise that never quite materializes.

Word of the Day. Worthwhile. Driving a carpool is the surest way to get on the board.

SAM AND FOOTBALL

Last week the Rebels met the mighty Golden Hawks. The two great powers in the North of the River Tackle Football League Bantam Division. Titans, each.

Sam played on the Rebels. He is a compact tight end. He dreams, like all boys do, of making the play that will cinch the game.

The tone was set early. We had our lawn chairs, boom box and rap music. "Go girl, go girl, go girl."

We did not fear the Golden Hawks, nor they us. We did, however, get a little wet behind the knees when we saw the balloon arch on their side of the field, a snappy banner and matching red jackets worn by coaching staff and parents alike. The Hawks were so organized that in their prayer huddle, each boy had a speaking part.

When the Golden Hawks, parents and Nike representatives met after the game, it lasted for 20 minutes, or longer than time of possession for the Rebels. Had the Hawks risen off the turf like their lovely balloons, we would not have been surprised. Everything else they tried worked.

We lost, but not for a lack of coaching. The Rebels have four able coaches—police officers (our best chance would have been to arrest the opposing quarterback for trespassing on our pride and dignity) — along with 42 assistant coaches, or 1½ per player. The assistants, when they weren't drawing military coups in the dirt, roamed the sidelines yelling instructions to the players, coaches and people in the neighborhood out for a breath of fresh air after dinner.

As invigorating as the game was the playful repartee between assistants and head coaches.

"You guys might as well be cheerleaders for the Golden Hawks," shouted an assistant to the coaches when they didn't protest a somewhat questionable call by the officials.

"We're doing the best we can," the coach yelled back.

Sam, like all tight ends, has imagined himself slanting across the middle, catching the ball and running for a touchdown. This might be possible on some teams, but the Rebels were gifted with Lyle, the 90-yard junior Olympic sprint champion at halfback. He had a way of making the secondary look as if they were running on legs the size of cribbage pegs.

Sam, a persistent boy, both home and away, convinced the coaches to add a play. Practices toward the end of the year were happy ones because he would say, "Mom, they ran my play in practice today."

"Dad, I think they're going to run my play tonight," he said, before the last game with the Golden Hawks.

This would have been a good time to do it. Sam's family was there as well as his out-of-town grandfather.

In the third quarter, on second and 10, when the Rebels were down 13-0, the quarterback dropped back in the pocket and threw to No. 89.

No. 89 had it in his hands for a moment, but the ball dropped to the ground. The pass had been behind him. So says Sam, Sam's agent and a host of impartial witnesses unlikely to change their story.

"Dad, they called my play tonight," Sam said after the game as we walked to the car.

He smiled. It was the kind of smile that catches you off guard. That's when I knew, regardless of the score, we had a winner.

SNOW

By 6 a.m., the neighbors had made four snowmen. They were building an army. Breakfast, wet feet, numb hands, nothing could stop them.

Our youngest has been asking lately, "Will it ever snow in Bakersfield?" We shake our heads, give specific explanations, talk about rainfall, altitude and location. We have a thousand reasons why. Monday was a victory for the why nots. A victory for believers.

I've seen snow twice in my 40 years here. Both times, the experience was meteoric. It was over in seconds.

Not this time. It fell, it stuck, it stayed, and we have pictures to prove it.

What pictures. Trees being weighed down with snow. The Volvo with two feet of the white stuff on the hood. A snowplow rumbling up and down Truxtun. Branches snapping like pistol shots.

Did you notice how many people were up at 3, 4, 5 in the morning? A friend in the Panorama area said he encountered neighbors he had never seen. Not only did he see them, but they were friendly. Snow turns out to be the great ice breaker.

Usually, it's impossible to get kids up before 6. They grumble, they roll over, they play dead.

Not Monday. They sprang out of bed like it was Christmas. Within minutes of putting on shoes, sweatshirts and jeans, they were in the streets.

Snow is quiet, not pleasantly noisy like the rain. More than quiet, it's beautiful. Bakersfield has never looked better.

"Awesome," said the guys at Jim Burke Ford at 6:30, staring through the chain link fence at Beach Park where children were sliding down the banks.

I heard the word "awesome" 50 times. I used it 25. It wasn't enough. It couldn't describe what Monday morning was like. It was as close to a miracle as most of us are going to get. After this, you might as well roll the credits.

Who didn't get a call early Monday morning? Get one or make one? Normally these are disaster calls. The "who died" type.

Not Monday. Those were "good news, Charlie" calls. That was like telling somebody they'd won the lottery.

By 5:30, it seemed as if the whole neighborhood was in the streets. One man running; a couple walking, wearing wool hats that hadn't seen daylight since Greenhorn; others driving around slowly.

It was no time to sleep. You could sleep another 30 years and not see this.

We had an impromptu breakfast at a friend's house. The hostess said, "Life as we know it has been cancelled." If it feels that good to cancel life for a day, what would it be like if we called it off for a week?

Bakersfield is good for one of everything. A shark's skeleton on top of a dusty hill. Floods that would make the Bible proud.

Monsoon rains, the Virgin Mary appearing on the side of a house, a 100-foot-high cactus, the worst possible murders imaginable, winds capable of carrying Dorothy back to Kansas.

Monday's snow had them all beat. It made all the disasters and the other impressive feats of nature seem inconsequential. It covered power poles, cars, trees, and, for a moment, our sins.

Not that we had any. Not that they aren't going to be back tomorrow. That's OK. For a few hours, we were clean.

It was great. For a day, our town looked like Innsbruck. Bring on the winter Olympics. We wouldn't have to bribe a soul.

QUITTING HISTORY DAY

The house hasn't fallen down.

The kids aren't shooting heroin yet. There are no signs that our lives are unraveling.

We quit soccer.

We quit History Day.

We Lived.

Three weeks ago, we were just another overbooked, overcommitted, overwrought American Family. With school, with extracurricular activities, and with sports. We were chasing our tails. Then one day, light broke through.

"Dad, I want to quit soccer," Thomas said.

What do you mean you want to quit soccer? Haven't you read our press release? This is not the kind of family that quits soccer. We work the ball downfield, set up the shot and then kick it through the net.

Quitting.

What about the speech? The one about the dangers of quitting. The speech my dad gave me, the one his dad gave him, and the one — I'll be proud, son — that one day you'll give your children.

Do you know what happens to quitters, son? Their teeth go bad, most of them end up with an incurable case of yellow fever and many live in maximum security prisons.

No, "quit" is not in our vocabulary.

A few years ago, a friend from college was in a bad marriage. He told me he was thinking about leaving the marriage (no kids). He asked my opinion.

Divorce? Unthinkable. You stay in that marriage and be miserable like the rest of us.

"I think we ought to let Thomas quit," said Thomas' mother. "If he doesn't we'll have a soccer practice four nights a week and we'll never have a family dinner again."

Sleeping with the enemy. Suddenly, I had two quitters on my hands. On the grave on my dead grandfather, I could let this happen.

I asked the child if he was ready to cover the registration fee if we're not able to get a refund. I asked him if he were ready to forgo organized sports not only for the year but perhaps for the rest of his life.

Yes, yes, yes.

"Dad I just want to play with my friends in the neighborhood," he said.

That night, I called the soccer coach. I started the conversation by telling him what a great coach he was. I told that I agreed with this coaching philosophy, that I admire his commitment to soccer.

Then I dropped the bomb. He was fine. I was a mess.

A week later, Thomas' brother quit History Day. We were on a roll. My daughter came home, complained about tennis. I told her she could quit that, too. She acted surprised. Don't be. The cork is off the bottle. The genie of quit is free.

Life is still busy.

I love soccer, but have we missed it? No. I love History Day, but do we miss it? No.

It takes everything Thomas' mother and I have not to high five each other as we pass one another in the hall.

Thomas comes home from school. He has a bowl of cereal. Does his homework. Then he puts on his bike helmet, gets on his bike and rides off to meet his friends in the alleys where bike ramps, chase and capture games and general hanging around awaits. It's a pretty good life for a kid, or any other person with common sense.

My friend from college isn't doing badly either. He got divorced and remarried. He has a terrific family and is doing well.

Doing well just like the rest of us quitters.

CHARLES WERNER

Every so often, Charles Werner speaks to his wife six feet under and says, "Honey, don't tell Thelma I'm a gardener."

Thelma is like family. She lies next door to Carol Sue Werner — "Beloved Wife, Mother and Grandmother" — at Greenlawn Cemetery.

Charles, a 63-year-old Willie Nelson look-alike, is very particular about the appearance of his wife's grave. That explains the "don't tell Thelma I'm a gardener" line. As if she doesn't know.

"As long as I'm living, I want this to look nice," said the one-time refinery worker with an unlit cigar clenched backward in his teeth so people know he's not smoking. "After I'm gone, it'll be up to somebody else."

His wife, a longtime employee of Contel, died March 31, 1994, of heart problems. The couple had been married 39 years and four months. Charles has been to her grave almost every day since.

Charles has a routine. He arrives around noon with a 5 gallon bucket. Inside the bucket is a 4-inch Sears cordless electric grass shear that he bought on sale for $39, a 20-foot hose, a Yuban coffee can that holds an insulated coffee cup flush to the ground, two pairs of household scissors, a pair of hand shears, a soft medium bristle brush, a hand towel, an 8-foot piece of string with a nail on each end, a bag of grass seed and a tape measure.

"The first thing I do is give her a drink of coffee. I pour it right on her grave. I say, 'Here, you are sweetheart.' In the summer, I give her a sip of iced tea, too.

"Then I turn the bucket over, sit down and shoot the bull with her. It's kind of like meditating. I think about the good times. I tell her about going to Marie Callender's the night before, or waxing the kitchen floor."

While meditating, Charles is studying the gravesite to see whether any new weeds have come up. The minute he stops meditating, he pounces on the weeds. Meditation is one thing, weeds are another.

In the spring, he scatters grass seed on the bare spots. Wednesdays, he mows the area around his wife's grave, and the one he will someday occupy. With the string and two nails, he makes sure he's cut a straight line.

After watering, he wipes the headstone with the hand towel. Worn, weathered or stolen red silk rose buds are replaced with new ones. A while back, he dug out a perfect symmetrical 12-inch-by-12-inch heart into the grass over his wife's plot.

Not that Charles is totally fixated on his wife's 3 ½ -foot-by-8 ½-foot piece of land. Over the three years he has adopted 15 grave sites, some close to his wife's. As a man might buy a rental next door to prop up his own property values, so has Charles taken over the care of several graves in the immediate vicinity so that their beauty will enhance his wife's.

Charles, who speaks with a strong southeastern Missouri accent, is not lonely. He is friends with the groundskeepers and others who visit the cemetery. People like Carol Knapp, manager of Wells Fargo near his home in Oildale, drive by almost every day and honk.

Occasionally, he prays. Sometimes for his wife. Mostly it's about the gophers.

"I ask the good Lord, I say, 'Please don't let them dig where I mowed.' "

So far, they haven't.

GOOD BABYSITTER

A good baby sitter makes an average husband disposable. Especially if she sweeps, bleaches the sink and picks flowers from the garden and arranges them on the kitchen table.

We are losing our baby sitter of 10 years. She's concocted some fantastic sounding reason — like she wants to continue her education at the university.

Imagine, pursuing a career that pays four times what we pay doing something other than watching our children two days a week.

Amy started baby-sitting when she was 12. Our youngest was just a baby. The older three were 8, 6 and 4.

Common sense tells you that our baby sitter needed a baby sitter herself, but not Amy. From the start, she was composed, in charge and carried off her duties with an air of prepossessed authority.

She practically raised Thomas. She could stop him crying when nobody else could. His earliest memories, when he becomes an adult and reflects back on his childhood, will no doubt include her. Amy and the Happy Face cookie she bought him once a week from Smith's.

Amy was the standard of feminine beauty for our daughter, who is four years younger. In matters of taste, appropriate clothing and fashion, Amy's voice carried weight. She knew what would look good on an 8 year-old girl, a 10 year-old, 12, 14 and 17, and she knew where to get it.

Through her, the kids learned about the mysteries of shopping the discount stores, Goodwill, the joys of a $2 Hawaiian shirt, a $1.50 pair of extra-long shorts. From her, they learned that frugality was not a dirty word.

She filled the house with flowers. Spring, summer and fall. I'm a guy. I don't notice those things, but Amy broke Sue's heart with joy with the fresh sweet peas, roses and other blossoms artfully arranged.

In the fall, she made a fall wreath; in the winter, a winter one. She made creativity seem like the most natural thing in the world. School projects requiring an illustration or diorama were a snap for her. She was one of those people who could turn scraps from the ribbon drawer into a work of art.

The house was always cleaner than we had left it. Amy had a way of scrubbing the sink and counter until it gleamed. Amy had her secrets and she's taking them with her.

Call home and she'd answer. For a mother who hated to be away from her kids, this was close to being there herself. Amy was a better anxiety depressant than Prozac.

Pre-formal jitters? Amy was there to apply the makeup, style the hair and calm the formal-goer's mother.

As the kids got older, the notes she wrote detailing the day's activities would become longer, noting transgressions rather than accomplishments. She was as much out of the baby phase as we were. She wrote the long notes, we understood the long notes.

It sounds terrible, I know, I don't mean it like this, but she's going to make somebody a great wife. Not just a great wife, a great friend, a partner and a mother. It's not just a matter of having the skills. Amy is lovely in the ways that count.

Without knowing it, she's left a permanent wreath on the door. It says, "I cared for your children." The wreath cannot be taken down and will not be forgotten.

AFTER SHOWER

Awhile back, I asked one of the boys to sweep the deck. This does not fall under the category of news. Nor under the category of surprise. Nor punishment.

Sweeping the deck is a weekly activity well within the realm of appropriate teen-age tasks. The leaves grow. The leaves die. The leaves fall.

Some fall on the ground. There is poetry to leaves falling on the ground. Leaves falling on decks lack that poetry.

"Dad, I can't sweep the deck, I've already taken my shower," he responded.

Stop the presses. Shut down the nuclear power plants. Tell the toll keepers to stop taking quarters on the Bay Bridge. Prince Charming has already taken his shower.

Let me set the scene here. This is not 6 p.m. on a school night. Not 6 p.m. on a work day. No one has studied hard or toiled long.

It's 9:30 Sunday morning. The child in question just woke up. It's nice to rinse off in the morning. No one's saying it isn't. People like their morning shower. It can be a boost. A way to freshen up before church, before brunch, or before visiting a friend's new baby, but none of these activities had been scheduled.

We weren't going anywhere. We had not been invited anywhere. Presumably, in lieu of invitations that had not materialized, one of the things we might choose to do is work on the house. We live in the house — sometimes it makes sense to work on the house. Sweep, water, dust or paint. Any or all would do.

The idea is not to lay the shower blame on one child. Other members of the family share the same affection for the cleanliness gene. They are quick to invoke the power of the shower.

In our house, you'd think that showers have the same milestone effect that the birth of Christ had in terms of history. Before Christ was one world. After Christ another. At home, the milestones are A.S. (after Shower) and B.S. (before Shower). With B.S., anything is possible. In A.S., the world shrinks. Possibilities vanish.

It's not as if nothing can happen in the A.S. world, because it can. Light ironing is possible. Breakfast. E-mailing. A phone call or two, a crossword puzzle. A.S. may even include doing a sinkful of dishes.

A.S. becomes less flexible, though, when it includes the statement, "But I've washed my hair." Hair is sacrosanct. Once hair enters a conversation, the possibility of work diminishes. The only thing left to do is make reservations at your favorite restaurant, play gin rummy or talk about the presidential election.

I had a friend in college who took five showers a day. He was constantly in a state of A.S. but it wasn't as critical. If he took a shower, you knew he was going to follow it with another shower. Each activity, sweat producing or not, was punctuated with a shower. He called it rinsing off. After he'd rinsed off, he'd start something else (not necessarily strenuous either). As long as the hot water held out, his life moved forward in waves of clean anticipation.

Perhaps this is the solution. Demystify the shower experience. Encourage more showers. Punctuate work with showers—and maybe we can sweep the leaves off the deck.

BIKING AND THE ART OF SAYING GOODBYE

I asked her to vacuum and for once, she didn't. Willful? No. She just forgot. Or never heard me. She had other things on her mind.

I didn't say anything. I guess I had other things on my mind, too.

The week before your first child — your oldest, your only girl — leaves for college, may not be your best week together. A friend told me why:

"She's trying to convince herself that she's ready to go," she said. "In order to do that, she has to believe there is no way to get along with you any more."

I'm convinced. Now be who you were before we entered the tunnel of separation and independence.

In her quieter moments, I've caught her staring into the distance. What does she see?

I'd like to think she was contemplating the grace with which she's lived most of her life. Or that she was giving thanks for her wonderful parents.

It was probably neither. Most likely she was wondering what Internet service she was going to be hooked up to at college.

Last Monday, we went to her favorite Mexican restaurant. We've had good times at El Pueblo in Lamont when she was younger. She looks at Lamont as the mecca of Mexican food.

"Dad, do you think I'll be able to get good Mexican food up north?" she said.

Probably not. Getting decent Mexican food up north is like finding redwoods in Mojave. Mexican food is good only in your hometown.

Last week a friend came by, and, finding Katie still there, proposed a neighborhood farewell party.

Like many families, we've drunk deeply of our neighborhood, and it has sustained us through good and bad. Now, we look for it to work its magic again.

Days before leaving, she was busy. A pedicure on Tuesday at the beauty college for $10, her hair trimmed on Wednesday. Then Thursday, she went to lunch with a friend. I don't know how she managed it all.

Busy as she was, one night she asked her mother if they could go through the photo albums so she could take a few pictures with her. Two hours later, they'd gone back two years and she'd selected 60 pictures of her grandparents, cousins and family and familiar haunts like Mammoth and Del Mar.

Everybody manages in their own way. I spent more time than necessary getting her bike ready. New tubes, new bike lock, three extra tubes in case of flats.

I did this knowing that she'd never appreciate any of it and that the bike will most likely get stolen or be left somewhere by Thanksgiving.

No, I didn't do it for the usual reasons: usefulness, responsibility, generosity. I did it for myself. This is how I readied myself to send a daughter away. I cleaned her bike and pumped up her tires.

Her brother is already talking about using her sink and closet. He has her moved out already. She can't go soon enough for him.

Eighteen years ago, we threw a stone into a clear, cool, Sierra-blue lake. At first, the circles were small, but gradually they increased in diameter. Now, we can no longer see the outermost ring. This circle is moving beyond our diminishing vision.

The family room carpet is still unvacuumed. I'll probably do it myself.

Friends warned me. This is how some people manage, when they say goodbye.

ONE LAST DANCE

While cleaning out the U-Haul, I found the box with the extra tire tube in it. What happens if she gets a flat? It's only 300 miles. Should I run up to Davis? I could be home by dinner.

Last Sunday, we took our daughter to college. If you haven't gone through it, you may not want to sit through the preview. When the movie is released, I'd try to miss that, too.

There had to be a mistake. We were driving away from the campus, the U-Haul was empty and there were only five of us in the car. Katie was back in her fifth-story bathroom wiping away the tears.

Don't be sad. You have the new blender. We still have the old one.

Smoothies aside, I feel like a baseball pitcher who's gone seven and a half strong innings, throws a couple of balls to the backstop and looks up to see the manager at the mound, scuffing the dirt, with his hand out. Don't take the ball, I'm not ready to sit down yet.

We talked about this on the way home. When we could talk. When we weren't staring at a new life that we weren't quite sure was going to be an improvement over the old.

In your early years, becoming a parent is the last thing on your mind. Then you get married, have a child and realize that all you ever wanted was to be was a parent.

That's good. That's fine. That road is straight and stretches off into the distance.

That's what you think. That road was curving all along. Life is a circle. There might be a time when this symmetry will bring pleasure. This, however, is not one of those times.

As much joy as you feel holding your child the day they are

born, you may feel the corresponding measure of sorrow the day you take them to college.

I was talking to a father in the parking lot as we were getting ready to leave Davis. He was a few minutes away from saying goodbye to his only girl, too.

"When we ate breakfast this morning, my wife was crying," he said. "I asked her why. She said that 'This was their last breakfast.' "

I told him I knew what she meant. It all had a biblical feel to it. The night before we'd had supper and I expected Judas to show up.

I talked to a mother on the elevator as I was taking Katie's computer upstairs. I was looking for some comfort and this was the second child she'd seen off to college so I figured she must have had some experience.

"On my first one, I cried for three months before and three months after," she said.

I was talking to the wrong people. I'd wandered onto the Oprah Winfrey set and couldn't leave.

Fifteen minutes before we left Davis, the boys and I went to buy film and a 9-foot extension cord. The song "Dance With Me" was playing on the sound system. I couldn't get away from the schmaltz.

When we returned to the dorm, Katie and her mother were pinning photos on the bulletin board. Pictures of her brothers, friends, aunts, uncles and cousins, maybe even one of her parents. It was as peaceful between them as it had been in months. It reminded me of the tea parties they'd once had.

A few months ago, a friend sent me the song "Nancy (With The Laughing Face)," by Phil Silvers, who had written it for Frank Sinatra to sing to his daughter Nancy. One of my favorite lines is "She takes the winter and makes it summer. Summer could take some lessons from her."

In the U-Haul at home, along with the bike tire tube, I found a picture of Katie with a friend. They are dressed up. They are mugging for the camera. They are laughing.

POMEGRANATES

Last week Dolly Hei, my friend from Shafter, brought me a large fruit jar of pomegranate jelly. Deep purple, heavy and with a taste that is both sweet and tart.

I mention this not to lord it over anybody who doesn't have a friend from Shafter who presses her own juice and then turns it into the most delicious of all jellies, but to say it's that time of year again — pomegranate time. Pomegranate season, along with the end of the Kern County Fair, speaks to the coming of fall.

Make a case for apricots as the fruit of fruits. I won't stop you. Sun-sweet, satisfyingly simple to eat, they have no weaknesses except one.

Apricots are an anxious fruit, skittery as a rabbit and have the shortest of seasons. One Monday in June, they are ripe and the next Monday they are on the ground. We stare at them in disbelief. How could you? I've waited all year for you and now you do this?

Peaches are more sure-footed. They can last three weeks. They have more mule in them than rabbit.

Pomegranates last almost the entire fall. In that way they are like persimmons, an equally sturdy and mysterious fruit. Rain finally does them in, encouraging mold, but pomegranates will sit on the tree in perfect repose until November. Miss them at the end of September, catch them at the end of October.

Pomegranates have an ancient feel to them. A friend tells me Jewish people eat them during high holidays and have been eating them since they were slaves in Egypt. On Rosh Hashanah, when Jews are being judged by God and want to accumulate points in their favor, "they eat pomegranates as a symbolic gesture in the hope that their merits will increase like the seeds of a pomegranate."

Growing up, we had a pomegranate tree and then we didn't. The people across the street had a tree but they made jelly. The house down the street had hundreds of pomegranates and we preyed on that tree like locusts.

In doing so, our hands became sticky, our mouths red and our shirts tie-dyed with purple pomegranate juice.

Between the ages of 18 and 40, I was pomegranateless. No tree, no friends, no future. I would see pomegranates in stores, but they never looked happy. They looked out of place as if they had been captured in a war between two great kingdoms and sold into slavery.

How did you get to be so expensive? It didn't seem right to have to pay for pomegranates. It was like having to pay for cool, dry autumn air.

Several years ago, friends gave us a sweet pomegranate tree. The crop was modest to begin with — four or five pomegranates. This year the crop is huge, threatening, even after two prunings, to strip branches off the tree. The pomegranates are redder than old crawdads.

Pomegranates are not easy pickings. Grab one and risk being jabbed by rose-like sharp thorns. Grab one and risk grabbing the almost prehistoric-looking insects that plant themselves on the ripe fruit.

Pomegranate season means weekly pomegranate parties. These parties are best enjoyed with small neighborhood children who are building pomegranate memories.

To split a pomegranate, cast it on the sidewalk. Then peel away the white fibrous material that will reveal one glorious section after another. The sections are as inviting as a new field of powder snow. Eating a pomegranate is uncovering an almost endless series of surprises.

Some people chew the seeds and then spit them out. Others chew and swallow. Pomegranates are rife with texture so either way is satisfying.

As the weeks pass, the air gets cooler and the pomegranates sweeter. Their languorous season delivers us deep into fall, falling leaves and failing afternoon light.

As local teacher and writer Ann Williams once wrote, it calls "up memory after memory of the season that touches me most."

The season, to paraphrase Williams, toward which we have always been moving. Now it has arrived, and so have we.

RECLINER

Last Sunday, my wife and I went to a furniture store and looked at recliners. Many people call these La-Z-Boys or Barcaloungers, but I prefer recliner because it has a more agreeable sound.

"Make sure you see what he looks like stretched out all the way," a woman friend warned my wife, "because that's what you're going to be looking at every weekend."

It's a civil war. It really is. The battles are fought by the men who want them and the women who'd rather have an electric train set in their living room than a La-Z-Boy.

"I told my husband that he would have to get a second wife in order to have a recliner," said a friend.

Do a survey. How many men do you know who have a recliner in their living or family room? It is a club with few members and many applicants.

Given that a woman may be disinclined to showcase a man lying on his back with his head flopped to one side, his mouth open, and perhaps crumbs on a T-shirt that has crept north of his belly button, recliners can be the most nomadic of furniture. They travel from the family room to the bedroom, the bedroom to the basement, and the basement to the curb.

I know one woman who bought her husband a recliner for his birthday. I asked her where it was.

"It's in our bedroom," she said. "It didn't go with the floral pattern and garden theme in my living room."

Prior to Sunday's joint visit to the store, I did some reconnaissance so as to narrow the choices to two can't-miss chairs: Purple leather or an orange tweed fabric. I was flexible.

I sat down in the leather version as if a demonstration of its comfort would advance the sale. I pulled the wooden handle up and the feet component sprung out. Hello, mama. I'm home.

"What do you think?" I asked.

She was quiet, nearly still, except for an almost imperceptible shake of her head.

"Do you have a recliner that doesn't look like a recliner?" she asked the salesman.

Women want a recliner that looks like a rake, a shovel, a wheelbarrow. Anything that represents work or the chance that it might get done.

If it doesn't look like a farm implement, then they would prefer the recliner be disguised as a love seat, a new dining room table or a trip to Europe.

"We have some wingback chairs that fold into recliners," the salesman said.

Wingback chairs? You mean the ones with arms harder than park toys and backs straighter than a church pew?

Wingback chairs are the iron maidens of the chair world. Why don't I just sit in the back of a pickup going 60 on a canal bank?

"How about a nice soft chair with an ottoman?" she said.

An ottoman? I wouldn't have been the first guy who went for the ottoman fake. Men settle for ottomans when their recliner dreams are dashed on the rocks of domestic tranquility.

"The strategy here," a friend had advised me, "is to slip the recliner in as part of a larger purchase. You might have to get a love seat or an ottoman, too, so that she won't notice."

A couple days ago, a woman told me that her Uncle Pete died in his recliner.

"Those of us who are on the sunset side of the sky want nothing more than to pass the rest of our days in a recliner," said a friend trying to explain both Uncle Pete and the allure of the recliner.

Some women understand. One friend of my wife owned a Barcalounger before she got married.

"I think the only reason he married me was my recliner," she said.

That sounds like a man who has good taste.

SEPTEMBER AND THE FAIR

In September, the coming of the fair means more than sincere 4-H students raising 1,000-pound pigs.

Fair means that fall is almost here. The fair is the gateway between seasons. Warm prior to and cool after.

I had my fair reminder two weeks ago when it was much too hot to think about pigs, bunnies or deep-fried Oreos. Elinor Grant, volunteer for First Christian Church, called to say the men had started to make the caramel corn again.

Fair food fanciers know which caramel corn I am talking about. During the fair, the First Christian Church sells about 12,000 bags of caramel corn from its stand across from the hot tub people.

The fair is like Disneyland. Expensive, if you don't buy a bracelet, thrilling if you have kids and satisfying if you like to throw pingpong balls into goldfish bowls.

However, there is a familiarity and innocence about the fair that trumps the exquisite organization of Disneyland.

Innocent because one day you're watching the baby chicks hatching under the heat lamps and familiar because, the next day, you're exploring the solid pleasures of the midway with all its glorious and colorful humanity.

We lived about a mile from the fairgrounds when I was growing up. At night, I'd climb to the top of the pine tree and watch the Ferris wheel spin round and round.

One of my most memorable dates took place at the fair. I was in high school and had arranged a date — no, not a date, a semi-date. It was less a commitment than an understanding. Cora Amos and I had arranged to meet at the fair somewhere between the Hammer and Strasner's, home of the famous Pit Beef Take-Away Sandwich.

Cora, like many of the girls I semi-dated, was way out of my league, but from my perch at the top of the pine tree, hands sticky with sap, I believed or at least semi-believed that anything was possible.

I showed up at the appointed hour and began walking south on the road down the midway. I was styling in my orange corduroy bell bottoms that I had bought from Chess King in Valley Plaza.

I looked up and about 100 yards away, there was Cora, looking beautiful under the lights of the midway.

I almost ran. It was like one of those movies that lacked only the tall grass and a Tony Bennett soundtrack. At 50 yards, I knew it was Cora, but I also knew something else. Cora was with Bobby Triplett, a track and football star at BHS. Bobby had everything I didn't, including Cora.

I'm not sure I said anything as we passed. I may have raised my hand in a semi-salute. I just kept walking and walked through the back gates and home to my pine tree.

Years later, I saw Bobby on the sidelines at a BHS game. Sometime after that, I read his obit in the paper. I remember him under the blazing fair lights with a beautiful girl.

The fair is important. It's not just about one season in your life. The fair is about all of them.

CHILLIN'

What's up with 'chillin' anyway?

My son is chillin'.

I know this because I heard him tell somebody on the phone that he was. I try not to eavesdrop on my children's conversations, but with cell phones, phone space has become public space.

The language — chillin', kicking it, what's up — drives me crazy like I suppose ours it did our parents. It's the price we pay for having our parents pay the same price.

A-n-y-b-o-d-y can chill, but it helps to be under 30, underemployed and overworked. "Chillin'" is not only a goal, it's a lifestyle. The less activity, the better. Chilling brings to mind something you'd trip over in the quiet room at the morgue.

Chillin' is more sedate than "kicking it." Kicking it sounds like the stylish finish to a Western dance. Kicking it is what you do on your way to chillin'.

When someone is chillin', it is generally frowned upon for his or her parents to ask them to do something like wheel the trash toters to the curb. "Can't you see, I'm chillin'?," his prone posture might indicate. If the child has prefaced the chillin' with a shower, then he is out of bounds for any request.

Later that evening we received a call from our older son who lives in Los Angeles. Given that he is out on his own, his opportunities for chillin' have diminished. That didn't preclude him from asking his parents, "What's up?"

What's up? Do you mean what has happened outside the normal course of activity? Or do you mean have I done anything exciting as of late?

Although the expression is intended as an expression of

friendliness, I find myself becoming defensive. Should something have happened to me? If not, are you suggesting I should get some zip in my life?

Up is not all that it seems. If something is up, it may not be that up. And if it's up, before you know it it might go down.

In the past, up has meant unsolicited phone calls from schools and perhaps law enforcement agencies. Some of us have had enough up, now we're looking for down.

The next day, I walked into work and overheard one of my co-workers finish a phone conversation by saying, "Thank you so much." It sounded as if a kind stranger had called and offered to retire her mortgage. If not that, had pulled her children out of quicksand.

"Thank you so much," might be a good trend. One demonstrating that we are grateful in this occasionally harsh world for the smallest of favors. Our hearts, always soft, have become even softer.

Thank you so much for reading. Please excuse me so that I can chill. That's what's up with me.

RUN LIKE THE WIND

Her name is Tatum Holland and if you asked her, she'd tell you that she didn't like to run that much in P.E. anyway. Now, she doesn't have to ever run in P.E. again.

If asked to take a lap, she'll have a decent excuse.

Tatum's excuse is her right knee, which started hurting before Christmas. Three weekends ago, her knee became more painful. Painful or not, the show had to go on — History Day State Finals a week later in Pasadena.

Tatum, 15, and a great kid by any measure, had qualified for the finals of the senior group performance division with her partner, Brittany Rice. History Day tests students' expertise in projects, including group and individual performance, historical papers, exhibit boards, documentaries, posters and Web sites. Each year, the competition has a new theme. This year's was "Rights and Responsibilities."

Tatum and Brittany's project was called "Darkness Before Dawn: The Battle of Britain." It addressed America's responsibility during World War II, specifically the decision about when the United States should have entered the war.

The girls interviewed 16 primary sources, Royal Air Force pilots, English people who lived through the Battle of Britain, and Andy Rooney of "60 Minutes." Along with the 500-word essay each team had to produce, the girls had done research at Stanford's Hoover Institution Archives and compiled a 29-page bibliography. They also had to write and perform a 10-minute skit.

Tatum comes from good History Day stock. Last year, she was a member of the national champion group performance team from Fruitvale Junior High, coached by Dan Peeler. As a seventh-grader,

Tatum had been a silver medalist.

History Day teams generate their own lives. Because of the enormous amount of research done and the often emotional topics undertaken — Holocaust, Vietnam, World War II, etc. — team members and their coaches and parents draw close. It's not unusual to hear participants talk about their History Day "families."

From Saturday's opening rounds, Tatum and Brittany emerged as one of the two top teams, which placed them in the finals later that evening.

The week before the competition had been a busy one, not only with last-minute additions to the bibliography and polishing their performance, but with tests. Medical tests.

Tatum's right knee continued to hurt and what her parents Greg and Janet initially thought were growing pains, turned out to be something else.

Thursday, two days before the competition, Tatum had an MRI and CAT scan. Friday, she had a bone scan. Her parents knew their daughter's condition might be serious, but decided not to tell Tatum the day before she and Brittany were to compete in Pasadena.

"I had talked to her brother," Greg said. "I knew he was worried because he started to be nice to her."

The girls nailed their performances in the finals on Saturday night. They would find out at an awards ceremony Sunday morning if they were one of the two top teams that would go on to nationals in June at the University of Maryland.

It would be difficult to find a venue tenser than the Pasadena Auditorium that morning as the results of the judged competition were being announced.

First the alternate was announced and when it was not 2,404, Tatum and Brittany's number, they knew they were going to nationals or going home.

Then the presenter read, "2,404." Both the girls cried. Tatum and Rice were heading to Washington. They'd been working since September.

Tuesday, the test results from the MRIs and bone scan revealed that Tatum had osteosarcoma in her right knee, a rare form of cancer that usually hits young males. Only 100 people in the United States and 8,500 in the world will contract osteosarcoma this year.

There would be no trip to nationals.

Tatum's reaction was predictable. A hard cry followed by an even harder one when she realized she wasn't going to be able to make the trip. She also wasn't happy about losing her hair, "every one" of them, the doctor had said.

Tatum never asked, "Why me?" Greg said. "She has faith that God is using her to spread his love."

Faith or not, tears flowed in the waiting room after the oncologist had given the diagnosis.

"We were standing there and an angel came to me," said Tatum, as casually as she might describe a neighbor dropping in for a cup of coffee. "A man looked at our group and came over to us and said, 'Can I pray for you?'"

After consultation with the oncologist, Tatum is facing three months of chemo to knock the size of the tumor down, then an operation to remove it, reconstructive surgery on her knee, then six more months of chemo.

The surgeon from UCLA who will be doing the surgery can save the leg as long as Tatum doesn't break it in the next couple of months.

History Day is never far from Tatum's universe. One of the first acts of business was to contact the alternate team from Clovis and tell them they were going to Washington. Then Tatum and Brittany wrote them a good-luck letter.

No. 2 on the list was forming a team for next year. The theme is "Exploration, Encounter and Exchange." Typically Tatum starts working on next year's History Day Project the day after the competition is over. This year is no different.

There is no school in the world that wouldn't rally around a kid like Tatum, and certainly not any in the Valley, the cradle of caring in California. Meals have been prepared. Prayer chains organized, linking church to church. Buttons have been produced with "Team Tatum" on them.

Liberty High School and Fruitvale Junior High have started a fund to help buy her a laptop computer and all the accessories so that Tatum, who will be five credits ahead at the end of this year, can keep up with her studies and graduate with her class.

After hearing the diagnosis, Coach Peeler and his wife, Susan, went to visit Tatum.

"Susan and I went over to strengthen her resolve and she did the opposite. She strengthened ours," Peeler said.

Tatum is already looking forward to P.E. with her friend Cassie in special ed class. Tatum doesn't have to run anymore.

Given her life and her friendships, when she walks again, she will not walk alone.

DOG ON ROOF

Friends were trying unsuccessfully to reach their out-of-town daughter.

They left several messages, which went unreturned.

"We called and told her the dog had climbed up on the roof," her mother said.

Within five minutes, the phone rang.

"You really had me worried," said the concerned child, after realizing that the dog on the roof had been a ruse in order to get her attention.

"Please don't do that again."

Why? It worked. Next time, the dog will have taken up the flute or be learning French.

We are not nosy. We really aren't. We want nothing more than to settle into the highlight portion of our children's lives.

However, getting there is tricky. First, they have to make it through mean landlords, expensive apartments, student poverty, entry-level jobs, empty refrigerators and breaking down by the side of the road.

In other words, being 20, 25, 28 or as long as it takes to see almost every kind of disaster at least once.

Parents have already experienced these delights themselves and are not in a hurry to go through them again, but parenthood is a game of reruns. You make mistakes and then you watch your children repeat them.

With cell phones, we know more about the wrinkles in our kids' lives than we bargain for. Knowledge gives birth to expectation, which gives way to alarm when children go radio silent. When people wrote letters, challenges often righted themselves in the time it took to answer the letters. Cell phones present no such buffer zone.

"She calls, she cries, she hangs up and she feels better and I feel awful," a mother once told me.

The hysterical phone call sometimes begets a follow-up call from parents. How are things going? Are you feeling better?

"No, mom, I'm fine," the child often says. "Why would you think otherwise?"

Why? Because the last time we talked to you, you were about to jump off the Golden Gate Bridge. That's why.

Recently, I was trying to reach one of our children. Several messages went unanswered. The child's mother picked up the phone and took a whack at it herself.

"Something has happened at home that we need to talk about," she said, leaving the message on her daughter's voice mail.

"Please call."

We had a call back in 30 seconds.

"I thought somebody had died," she said. "It sounded like something was really wrong."

Yes, something was wrong. We were driving ourselves into a froth trying to get in touch with you.

Fudging the truth might be the way to go. The possibilities are endless:

"Your mother and I are considering a trial separation. Your thoughts, please."

"Your grandparents mentioned inheritance for their grandchildren. Is this something that is important to you?"

"Is it too early to talk about your Christmas present?"

"Your brother is moving into your old room."

If none of these work, tell them that the dog is on the roof.

PING-PONG POW

Advised to spend more time with the teen-age boys, we are playing Ping-Pong.

A birthday netted one of them a Ping-Pong table. It was a hit. Not only is it a magnet for the neighborhood, but it is an opportunity to relax with family and friends.

Did I say "relax?" Ping-Pong is the crack cocaine of racket sports. It's addicting, potentially explosive and can destabilize a family quicker than a puff on a pipe.

Playing Ping-Pong is the gaming equivalent of dentistry. Close-up work in the smallest of venues. If you aren't bug-eyed at the beginning of a match, by the time it's 18-16 you are foaming at the mouth.

The games start slowly. The warm-up can be friendly. Lazy. The contestants chatting away, acting as if the furthest thing from their mind is blood.

Don't be fooled. The warm-up is to the match what the German-Soviet nonaggression pact was to World War II. Subterfuge. The beginning of a very long end.

Yes, Ping-Pong is war. As kids we played at the Bakersfield Racquet Club, leaving behind a string of shattered paddles, walls with gaping holes and mountains of crushed balls. After we were done, the club elders finally condemned the Ping-Pong room and removed the table. It was either that or bring in the wrecking ball.

It's hard to know what the final count was, but there wasn't a player among us who didn't feel as if he hadn't won at least one more game than his opponents.

Winning becomes trickier when the opponent is one's own child. Do you let him win? Do you let him win, say, 12 points, with the thought being that 12 points constitutes a moral victory?

The alternative is to beat him as badly as you can. Shatter his confidence and crush his spirit so he can learn the lesson that "life is like that."

One thing you don't want to do is lose, no matter which lesson plan you choose.

Losing in Ping-Pong is a slippery slope.

First, you lose a game in Ping-Pong; then your children are beating you regularly; the next thing you know they're eating your favorite cereal, staying out past curfew and ordering the steak at Luigi's.

This, I realize, stands in opposition to the tradition of passing the baton, letting the next generation take over. But I don't want to lose to my kids in anything, now or 40 years from now. They can wait until I'm dead to take over.

The matches, given a certain amount of stubbornness on both sides, are intense, emotional and not the least bit collegial. They are often punctuated with walls being punched, paddles being slung and language being fractured.

My advice is, when you buy a table, buy a punching bag too. A punching bag will save hands and spare walls.

Yes, we are spending more time together as a family, and accordingly, have experienced a communication breakthrough. Glaring at one another has replaced the awkward silence that grips much of the parent/teen-age interchange. Soon, we will be speaking.

We are on our way to passing the baton. I can sense the grip. Somebody just has to let go.

PRETTY IN PARIS

Coming from a bistro one evening, we saw three men sitting on a bench getting ready to open a bottle of wine. They were Russian, gracious and although I'm sure there is a much nicer word for it in French, they appeared to be winos.

The bottle had a cork in it, one of them held a corkscrew and each of them had a wine glass. Only in Paris.

We recently returned from Paris. Even for Paris, Paris is surprising. Surprising in a good way. It's easy to see why people fall in love.

I've never seen such style. The Italians may be better looking, but no one can out-dress the French. A Parisian woman can accomplish more with a scarf than most women can with a whole outfit.

Forget about the French models. The prettiest girl you'll ever see will be selling tickets at the Louvre handing out towels in the gym or selling chocolate pastry at the corner bakery. In America, she'd have an agent, a film and rows of adoring fans.

Dressing up is in the air. I was in the elevator of the hotel one day going to the gym. I stood next to an English woman in her late 50s who was wearing a beautiful gray suit.

"Aren't you a little underdressed for Paris?" she observed, looking at my shorts and Best Cabinets T-shirt.

She wasn't being rude, she was being instructive. It was her way of saying, "Remember where you are."

My brother Courtney got into the spirit of chic by accusing me of wearing the same red polo shirt two days in a row. Was is it not possible for a man to have two red polo shirts? It's not that red anyway, I'd say it was maroon.

A couple of days into the trip, we visited the Louvre, the great museum with more than 300,000 pieces of art. The Louvre is daunting because of its size—laid out straight it would be 10 blocks long. It requires making decisions.

The Winged Victory of Samothrace, the great sculpture, is a must, but after that, everything else is on the block. I decided to ignore all the little paintings and anything made of iron and clay.

That worked for a while, but after a couple of hours, I started skipping the big paintings too and anything from China. I blew off the Mona Lisa on general principle. By the end, I concluded that most paintings look better if you are sitting down.

The Musee d'Orsay is the more manageable museum. The former train station has a healthy collection of Renoirs, Monets and Millets as well as other Impressionists. You know you're in the presence of great art when your feet stop hurting, you lose the desire to sit down, and you remember what it felt like to be 9 years old and seeing your first shooting star.

Paris is one of those "Oh my God" cities. Just when you think you've seen the most stunning palaces, cathedrals and statues possible, it's time to go to Versailles. A 30-minute train ride from downtown Paris, Versailles is where the kings went in the summer before there was air conditioning and La Rosa bars.

I finally understood the French Revolution. Twenty-two thousand people worked on Versailles. They drained the ground, diverted a river, planted 3,000 trees, put in 150,000 bedding plants every year and installed 1,400 fountains and then had to look at it through the gates. Marie Antoinette dressing up as a milk maid was probably the last straw.

It's impossible to write about Paris and not talk about food. Parisians love food and especially chocolate. Visiting a chocolate shop in Paris is like going to church. There is the same quiet and feeling of reverence.

Denise Acabo, proprietor of Chocolaterie Confiserie, pointed to some candied almonds that only she made and said, "I am alone in Paris with these almonds." Then she pointed to the chocolate-dipped cherries and said, "I am alone in Paris selling these cherries." Selling chocolates can be a lonely business in Paris.

My sister-in-law described a conversation she'd overheard. A group of French people were talking, and she deduced from their heated tones that the subject was something serious like the merits of invading Iraq or the state of French culture. She asked a friend for a translation.

"They were talking about the health benefits of chocolate," she said.

They could have been talking about trash cans and it would have been worth eavesdropping because anything sounds good in French. The three-minute safety speech on the airplane sounds like music in French. Somebody can tell you to jump off a cliff and you'd do it, as long as the instructions were in French.

The only thing prettier than the language is the music. Some of the best music in Paris is in the Metro and on street corners. I heard a single French horn playing Vivaldi, a Latin American group called Cenizas that featured flutes, guitars and joyous harmonies and a man playing tenor saxophone that made you think of Coltrane.

On our last night in Paris, we sat at dinner next to a couple in their early 60s. It wasn't long before we were sharing food and toasting each other with the house beaujolais. Over dessert, the woman told us she had always liked Americans. She said her father had been killed by the Germans. She thanked us for what we had done during World War II. Then, she told us she appreciated us for coming to Paris.

It was surprising, heartfelt, and like the music on the Metro.

HERBIE'S ROOM

The blue Bible rested on top of the biography of Kurt Cobain. Kurt Cobain. The Bible. If that doesn't describe a teenage boy. They can't decide whether to kill themselves or get down on their knees and pray.

Last week, I started painting my son's room. In order to do that, I had to move his books, clothes, posters and the soft guitar case out of his room. I found the Bible his mother had given him and the Cobain biography.

Herbie, now 20, moved to L.A. a year ago to pursue a career in music, which has included a career working in a music store, a career folding clothes at Abercrombie and Fitch Co. and a career cleaning carpets. Has there ever been a clear path to the artistic life?

We are in a transition stage with our children, two of them having left home. Although my inclination is to take those rooms down to the studs, that is not the consensus in the house. There is a period of time, I have learned, where closets, rooms and dressers remain untouched. The room is a shrine and nothing can be allowed to break its spell.

We are through the mourning stage, but still the room has stayed intact. We have been avoiding it and not just for sentimental reasons. Who knows what we might find? Who knows how much damage might have been done to the infrastructure? Teenage boys are not known for their light touch.

I was not disappointed. Underneath the A Clockwork Orange poster featuring a grinning Malcolm McDowell was a jagged hole in the wall 2 feet wide by 3 feet long.

I had forgotten about the hole. He would have hardly been a 16-year-old boy if he hadn't punched a wall or attacked a door after being denied a privilege or a night out.

A clock frozen at 5:35 hung on the wall. A skateboard broken in half lay in the corner. A knotted tie and a brown braided belt lay on the floor. A rectangular metal sign, the kind you get at Smart & Final, hung on the door. It read "Caution! Teenager Parking only. All others will be towed."

The closet was stuffed with books like What is Meditation?, The Kidnapping of Aaron Green, One Hundred Years of Solitude, a compilation of the comic strip Zits, and The What's Happening to My Body? Book for Boys.

He had written "Abolish government" on the outside of his closet door. A poster called "America's Most Wanted" hung on the inside. It had photos of marijuana plant varieties known as K.B. Killer, Dutch treat and Purplecstasy. On a shelf in the closet was a bullet, a token for the Palace Entertainment and a quarter, three dimes and 16 pennies. I kept the money, but threw away the bullet and the token. I didn't want to redeem either one.

Trophies sat on one of the closet shelves. They included "Superior Performance History Day 1997," and "Outstanding Practice Saxophone 1993 Spring Recital."

This son normally did not do things for which trophies were awarded. If he performed an especially daring maneuver on a skateboard, it would have been most often met with a quiet nod from a friend.

"Save the trophies," his mother had said. "I want to dust them off and put them back on the shelf."

Taped on the wall was a Happy Birthday note from his mother on a piece of typing paper. In the center was a quote from Bruce Springsteen.

"It's the turn of the century, and I started thinking of where I want to be on that night. The answer is I want to be with the people I built my life around. I want to be with them on this stage doing this thing. It's one of the greatest things I can do."

I saved the Bible, the Cobain biography and the birthday card. They are clues. One day, this son will return and we may know what they mean.

MY RAP CAREER

I read an article last week that said after 30 years of explosive growth, "rap music is now struggling with an unprecedented sales decline and growing criticism from within about the music's negative effect on youth."

Imagine my disappointment. Rap can't die yet. I haven't put out my first album. I'm bustin' with rhymes.

An aspiring rap star knows how critical the right producer is. I've got my eye on Dr. Dre because he is used to working with white guys. Dr. Dre produced rapper Eminem, who is whiter than Vanilla Ice, Billy Idol and Paul Bettany, the albino killer in The Da Vinci Code.

Another important factor in a successful rap career is being bad. I don't know if I'm bad, but I am unpredictable. I'm capable of anything.

I'll give you an example. The other day, I picked up the paper off the lawn and threw it on to the front porch. It bounced off the front door and almost hit the green mailbox on the rebound.

It was lucky for the woman who calls herself my wife that she wasn't opening the door at the same time. Otherwise, she could have gotten a bruise on her ankle that would have looked like a prison tattoo.

Prison's important. I drove by Wasco State Prison the other day. This cemented my reputation in the rap world in two ways: Not only was it a prison, but it was a drive-by. The only thing better would be if that prison had been in Compton.

If you're going to be a rapper, it's important to have treated your woman badly. I've done that. More than once.

The other day we had cross words. When she left the room,

I shot her a look. You should have seen that look. It would have peeled black paint off a barbecue.

Then, she made onion soup for dinner. There was enough left for a single serving for lunch the next day and she put dibs on it. Like dibs is going to stop me.

The next day at lunch, I opened the fridge and I glared at the Tupperware dish of onion soup. I didn't eat it, but I could have. You see, in my house, what I think may not go, but it certainly demands occasional regard.

Partying is important if you're a rapper. The other night, we had a dinner party and I stayed up doing the dishes until 11:10. That's late for a white rapper with four kids.

I have a stable of vintage automobiles, most from the early '90s. Some have tinted windows. They're somewhat low-riders, but that may have to do with tire pressure.

I can be distressed by the Man. When I get like that, I may be unwilling to play by the rules. A couple weeks ago, the men who pick up the recycling skipped a week. In protest, I left my blue recycling toter on the curb so that it got in the way of the street sweepers.

I don't have much jewelry, but every so often I'll leave a blob of shaving cream on my ear. People notice. Sometimes, they say things like, "That guy is wearing ice."

I am, I believe what they call, strapped. My arsenal includes rubber bands, Post-it notes and a blizzard of emails. That and a willingness to strike whenever my blood sugar is low.

That's how you roll when you're almost from Compton. You do it and you do it again.

SELLING THE CALIENTE SUBURBAN

A few days ago, a man came over to buy the Suburban.

I say "buy" because you can tell. He had that "I want to buy your Suburban" tone of voice. He also set a specific time at which he would arrive and he stuck it like a dismount by an Olympic gymnast.

Even though the sale was a sure deal, I wanted to give him the full monty. I hosed off the car, scrubbed it with a citrus-based cleanser and then rinsed it off again. After Windexing the windows, I rubbed the car with a chamois cloth.

The Suburban gleamed. It was like the sun pulling other planets into its orbit. The car was perfect.

Perfect, that is, except for the 2-foot long X somebody had keyed on the hood of the car. Perfect except the rear brake lights that had been knocked out of whack. Perfect except the dent in the driver's side door. Perfect, in other words, except that the car was 11 years old, had 167,000 miles on it and had seen its share of combat duty.

Shortly after 11, a new white Toyota SUV pulled in front of the house. That was a nice car. With a car like that, you don't need a car like mine.

Two men, one in a tank top and the other in a T-shirt, and two teenage boys piled out of the car. The older of the two boys, soon to be a student at BC, served as the translator for his father who was short on English but long on product knowledge. The father walked around the car several times. Although his expression remained serious, it was clear he was hooked.

"My father wants to know if he can look under the hood," the boy asked.

Sure he can look under the hood. I hadn't looked at the engine for a while, but I assumed it was still there.

"My father would like to know what these two hoses hook up to," said the boy.

I looked at the two hoses. I faintly remembered John, the mechanic, disconnecting them but I couldn't remember why. The car obviously didn't need them. I was surprised he didn't know that all Suburbans come with two extra hoses which may or may not be hooked up, depending on the driver's pleasure.

I asked him if he would like to drive the car, sensing that a change of subject matter might be in order.

"My father would like to know whether you want to go with him?" said the boy.

I told him it wasn't necessary. A white Toyota SUV and two teenagers qualified as sufficient collateral. I knew they'd return for at least one of them.

The two men stepped into the car. Ten minutes later, they returned. The father said something to the son. My Spanish was rusty but I did pick up the word caliente.

"My father wants to know why the engine is running hot," he said.

The engine is running hot? That's not possible. This engine never runs hot.

I popped the hood. No smoke or steam, that was good. I wrestled the radiator cap off and green water boiled out as if from a small, angry volcano. I told him that this had never happened before. I told him the radiator was new. I said some other things in the car's defense.

I might as well have been shouting into a storm. No one could hear me and those who could, didn't believe me.

"My father says he'll call you tomorrow after you've been to the mechanic," the boy said.

I stifled the urge to chase after the Toyota as it pulled slowly away from the curb like a dog. After a nice big drink of coolant, the car has run cool ever since. Naturally.

Friend Russ has a name for deals like this. He calls it quiotes. The word is from Oklahoma and Texas.

It means the deal is dead and there's no bringing it back. This Suburban was quiotes.

FIRST JOB

Our daughter recently got her first job. For most parents, this is a stand-alone sentence. First job. Independence. Out on your own.

I'm not even sure what it is she's doing. What it is that she is selling. All I know is that the name of the company she is working for ends in "ox" and it is based in Northern Ireland. Northern Ireland, a company that sounds scientific — what else does a parent need to know?

Prior to taking the job, there were conversations about salaries, commission structures, 401(k)s, and medical and dental packages. I don't remember having these conversations with my parents before I took my first job as a busboy at Jake's at the Beach in Santa Monica.

"You're offering me a job? I can make enough to buy a stereo? I'll take it."

Thirty years ago, you didn't think about insurance. You tried not to get hurt. You brushed regularly. You drank orange juice.

"Dad, what do you think I should do?" Katie asked, in reference to the company whose name ended in ox.

What do I think you ought to do? I think you ought to take the job. Who knows when another is going to come along? This could be the last job in the world and after this one, we might launch into another depression.

Don't let me appear too eager. Your mother and I have only be waiting 22 years for this day. We certainly don't want to rush you.

"Do you think the car allowance is enough?" she asked.

Car allowance? They're giving you a car allowance too? I'd say yes, since it's going to allow you to drive a car that is spiffier than anything your parents own. I'd say any car allowance is a good car allowance.

A new job in the family is like having a baby. Parents have a tendency to stand over the crib and coo. There is a honeymoon period the first couple of weeks as you appreciate the enormity of the event.

Some of the enormity has to do with the potential for education. You thought you learned a lot in college. How could you not, taking classes like communications, child psychology and European literature?

This is a different kind of learning. There is a short story called "In the Penal Colony" by Franz Kafka. Prisoners are put on a racklike contraption called a harrow that uses needles to tattoo whatever lesson their captors want them to learn. In the case of the condemned man in the story, the lesson was, "Honor Thy Superiors." Not a bad thing to remember when you've taken a new job.

The point is you learn things better when the lessons are tattooed on your back. Life after college is good for that. Soon enough you'll be on the rack, or on the freeway in rush hour traffic or on the outs with your best customer because someone beat your best price by 20 cents.

The learning, however, is not all needles and pain. You also learn how good it feels to make a sale, how satisfying it is to be making your own way and most importantly, how wonderful it is to have a raft of friends who will float you through the needles and pain part.

Katie — on the eve of your first job, I want to tell how proud I am of you. From baby to girl to woman, you've done it gracefully. And to think, you didn't even have a car allowance.

Being your father, I have some advice. Something I learned from the great columnist, Erma Bombeck. It's about using the good china.

Keep a bottle of champagne in the fridge. Celebrate along the way. When that bottle is gone, buy another.

SAM LEAVES

The week before Sam left, his mother gave him cooking lessons.

Monday it was pasta and chicken.

Tuesday — spaghetti carbonara.

The cooking lessons started at 5:30 p.m. He showed up on time. He listened. He was pleasant.

It's unclear whether his cooking repertoire extends beyond the two aforementioned meals, but Monday and Tuesday, he'll be as good as Emeril.

The cooking lessons reminded us that now there is one. This sounds like the title of a Dr. Seuss book rather than the description of a family which previously had four children living at home and now one remains.

Having one child at home is like not having any at all. The parenting load is light as a feather. We might as well be on vacation.

We've been waiting for this day and like most things posted in the future, it rarely goes as planned. Even when the child who is leaving home has walked on the wild side, you're still sad to see him go.

Minutes before he left, we sat in the living room. The living room, which has been part lecture hall, part holding cell and part war room. We have spent time there after midnight and past 2 and 4 in the morning wondering whether the evening would conclude with a knock on the door or a call from one of the law enforcement agencies.

That we made it thus far has had less to do with any expertise on our part than dumb luck. When everything else fails, a parent's best friend is the marathoner's creed: one more step. Faith helps too.

This time the living room was different. The sun was shining. School was out. The classroom was locked. The teachers had all gone home for summer.

This was goodbye. He was leaving. Going to San Diego for college.

His mother had a gift for him. Another gift? His father wondered what the last 18 years had been.

The present was less a gift than it was a symbol. A symbol of a mother's faith that cannot be discouraged, doused or dislodged. It is a faith in family, faith in children and faith that things will work out.

Things work out better when the working out also includes getting out.

His mother's gift was a cookbook called Help! My Apartment Has a Kitchen. Now, he could eat Wednesday through Sunday.

A week before he left, he drove to Visalia to have dinner with his grandparents. His grandmother served his favorite chicken dish, rice, salad and soft rolls.

Faced with cooking his own meals from memory and using unfamiliar cookbooks, food was becoming important to him. Food and cleaning supplies.

"I never thought I'd get so excited about cleaning supplies," he said to his mother after she brought home the basics to stock his apartment.

Fifteen minutes before he left, I washed his car windows. I was out of advice other than telling him to pack a bundle of rags. You can't have too many rags.

After Sam's first day of kindergarten, when he would have had his parents go to jail if it would have excused him from attending school, I remember being impressed by his resolve and independence.

"He will be the first one of our kids to smoke a cigar, move into an apartment and drive a Mustang convertible," I wrote at the time. "A tattoo is not out of the question. I can see Sam in the Navy, standing dockside with the wind ruffling his blond hair."

That same blond hair, longer now, swept in the warm summer breeze as he got in his car to leave.

"Stay out of trouble," he said to Thomas and his friends, who were gathered on the curb to say goodbye.

For Thomas, it was like getting advice from a pyromaniac on how to put out a fire. We would have laughed had we not been fighting tears.

And with that, he was gone. Has it really been 18 years? If so, what an 18 years it has been.

PERFORMANCE SKETCHY

Recently, I had my performance review. This is the once-a-year ritualized humiliation whereby the company filets your job performance like Gunther von Hagens does the human body in Body Worlds.

My performance review was five pages and took almost an hour. Was that 15 pages and eight hours?

If the company did not have a strict drug and alcohol rule, I would say that the best way to prepare for a performance review is to spend the night before working your way through a half-gallon of Old Granddad and quietly smashing your head against the wall.

Knowing that your review is approaching is worse than the review itself. It brings up every insecurity an employee has. Along with deep-seated paranoia.

"I know it would make a lot more sense to hire a 12-year-old and pay him in Skittles and root beer. That's what you're thinking, isn't it? I've seen you in your closed-door meetings, talking about me."

Paranoia leads to bitterness. "I've given my life to this company. I have nothing left. I am like a clam shell after the clam bake."

Bitterness gives way to melancholy. "What would I do if I got fired? I could teach, I suppose, but then I'd have to stand on my feet all day and I don't know if I can do that anymore."

There are sitting jobs and there are standing jobs. It's easier to go from standing to sitting than sitting to standing.

Melancholy turns to confusion. "Do they have any idea how much I mean to this company? If I were let go, this place would close the next day. Yet, do they ever say anything? I'm like a ghost around here. I might as well be the Brown Lady of Raynham Hall."

Confusion begets begging: "I realize I have a better chance of getting snatched by a pterodactyl and taken back to the nest to feed its young than I do of getting a raise, but please, please have mercy on me.

"I promise I'll do better next year. I'll start going to update meetings and cheering when someone else wins the raffle."

My strategy during the actual review is to keep my eyes fixed on the reviewer. I figure that if I am looking her in the eye and I am sincere about it, she cannot lower the boom.

The moment you look away, you're toast. This gives the reviewer the chance to load her gun and put her finger on the trigger. Look away a second time and the janitorial staff will be cleaning out your desk.

My other strategy is to never touch or read the review. This shows a certain independence and perhaps even confidence. It says, "I don't care what you say about me. I know who I am and I believe in that fiction."

I also try to compliment the reviewer. Tell her that even if everybody turned against her, that she could count me as a trusted confidant. I might add that I sympathize with the difficulty of her job.

"I know this is hard for you to do this," I say.

What I am thinking is. "You sadist, you're enjoying this."

What I say is, "I'm proud to be working with you."

I'm proud, proud I didn't wet my pants when you said, more than once, that I hadn't met expectations.

I'm proud that I'm still employed. I'm proud there is going to be a next time.

GOING TO BED MAD

Recently, a charming woman in her 70s was telling me about her late husband and their 50-year marriage. I asked her because I was curious, given the gentle demands of marriage, what her secret was.

"I never went to bed mad," she said. "Neither did he."

Never went to bed mad. How do people do that? Never going to bed mad is like never going to bed tired.

The don't-go-to-bed mad people are either better people than we are, more forgiving or they lack the good old fighting spirit.

There is only one way not to go to bed mad. Decline to take part in serious discussions after 8 p.m. As the evening progresses, grave talks have a way of becoming graver. If you feel the need to problem solve, do laps around the house.

Morning is best for those subjects that sometimes befuddle couples. Morning, "when the dew is on the meadow and the freshness is on the rose." When jovial couples can enjoy breakfast together and talk about the promising days ahead.

That is the goal, but some of us are moths to the flame and we find ourselves disgorging every little thing in our minds. As we soar into the fire of marital misunderstanding, the results are predictable. Evening conversations usually go something like this:

6 p.m.:

He: "I am glad to be home. I have had better days, but the last thing I want to do is take it out on my beloved wife or my family. This is my sanctuary."

She: "I am glad to see you. I know you are worried about money, getting fired and your son from your previous marriage who may be going to prison, but remember I'm with you on this. We're a team."

8 p.m.:

He: "My day wasn't bad, it was terrible. My boss pretends he has lint on his sleeve when I walk by. I'm not sure you understand me or what I'm going through. I lack contentment and I don't know why."

She: "Why? Because you are a big drip. Don't expect me to take a ride with you down Sourpuss Lane. You're on your own, prison boy."

9:45 p.m.:

He: "See. That's the way it's been our whole marriage — I've been alone. You know, you're lucky I'm not one of those guys who comes home drunk every night."

She: "I'm not sure I'd use the word lucky to describe myself. If there were a chance that drinking would improve your personality, I'd say cheers and bottoms up."

10:15 p.m.:

He says to nobody in particular: "I haven't been happy since college. What happened? Is this all there is?"

She says to her reflection in the wine glass: "Maybe it's time to get braces. I'm still young. I could be pretty again."

7:30 a.m.:

He: "I don't think you need braces."

She: "I accept your apology."

JOHN AND BEV MOVE TO BAKERSFIELD

Our children are leaving, but our parents may be coming.

I don't know what got into me. Middle-aged madness. A heretofore undetectable charitable streak.

My in-laws live in Visalia. I know the word "in-laws" can be loaded, the subject of countless jokes or insults depending on the context, but I don't feel that way.

I like John and Bev. Even respect them. John is retired, hasn't done a lick of serious work in about 20 years and he doesn't look the worse for it.

Bev's a saint. Part of it has to do with putting up with John. Plus, she makes homemade applesauce and occasionally lets her husband beat her in gin rummy.

I wrote them a letter. Their youngest grandson and I had been to Visalia for dinner, while my wife was in China. The letter was to thank them for dinner and to invite them to move to Bakersfield.

It's not that they're infirm, because they're not. They don't dodder and John doesn't walk around with applesauce on his chin.

Visalia is no reason to move either. Who doesn't like Visalia? It's Bakersfield without some of the mistakes. It's Bakersfield with the giant Sequoias at your doorstep.

However, Bakersfield has a grandson, Luigi's on Saturday, and empty streets on Sunday. "You did what?" said my wife, but I knew her heart wasn't in it.

She'd thought what I'd thought. That's what happens when you're married for a while. You think you have an original idea, but the person had it a week before you did.

"My parents have something to talk to us about," my wife said, several weeks later.

John and Bev were coming over for Mother's Day dinner. Bev was the guest of honor. Mother, wife, whatever, you want to call her, this woman deserved a statue of her own on the lawn.

It's funny having a serious talk with your in-laws. Compared to the kids, it's almost relaxed. What could they possibly say that would turn you inside out?

"As you know, Bev and I don't have long to live."

What? Your son-in-law invites you to move to Bakersfield and suddenly you're terminal. This is not good timing.

"What I mean is that we're going to be 80 pretty soon and who knows what's going to happen after that," John said.

Come on. Your mother, Bena, lived to 102. You can't go another 10 years? You could live another 10 years just hating Democrats.

"We're going to have to get a new roof," he said. "It's not going to be cheap."

That's why you called this meeting? To talk about your new roof and your terminal illness. When I wrote the letter, I had no idea it was going to cost you your life and $38,000.

Logic, heretofore in no hurry to present itself, finally emerged.

The house was too big. John was tired of doing the yard work. He'd gone from no kids, to no pool, to no yard. Pretty soon they'd be living in a treehouse.

They wanted to downsize, which involved putting on a new roof before they sold their house.

"When we retired, the last thing we wanted to do was throw ourselves on our kids," he said.

This was fun. I knew exactly where this conversation was going.

"We've looked at some cottage housing in Visalia," he said.

"But I think it's going to be noisy," Bev said.

OK, I thought, they wanted to know if it was all right to move to Bakersfield.

"Move here," I said. "We'd like to have you close. Then if you went down with your terminal illness, we wouldn't have far to drive."

No decisions were made that night. The door has been opened. The conversation ended and John was so relieved he had a couple glasses of wine. There's nothing he likes more than drinking his son-in-law's alcohol. If he moves here, I'll give him a key to the cellar.

HERBIE TURNS 21

The dinner started with a toast. Or perhaps it was a confession.

"I am happy to have made it to my 21st birthday," he said. "Many of my friends didn't."

There is joy in acing a test, starting a new job or falling in love, but everything pales next to the joy of finding yourself alive. The joy of having made it to a birthday, to an age and to a state of being that inspires gratitude.

That joy is especially intense when it is colored by the sadness of having lost friends one loved, ran with, laughed with and got stupid with; friends who weren't as fortunate. Friends lost at tender ages are remembered tenderly even as we age.

Herbie turned 21 recently. Our oldest son, our family's first grandson, was born on tax day.

His grandfather got a kick out of that. Tax day, that is. Given most people's lively relationship with the IRS, as far as he was concerned, Herbie might as well have been born on April Fool's day.

If April 15 had a humorous twist for us, it is that we found out the difference between raising boys and girls.

Our first son got stuck with the name Herb. Herb IV. It's one of those blessing/curses. It's the "A Boy Named Sue" syndrome. If you survive the funny looks you get much of your life, the jokes where the name is pronounced like garden herbs, there is a potential character building element to it.

The blessing is that Herbie's namesake, his grandfather, is a good man.

That's a lot to live up to. That's something to reach for, too.

Seasoned parents know that it's better to talk about their

children in reverse time. Looking back, rather than forward.

Not only is it safer, because the future can prove slippery, but it is also more satisfying.

If they are making it, if they are paying their parking tickets, then a parent can say without fear of retribution, "Things are improving. He has grown. He is turning (notice the use of the present participle) into a nice young man."

Yes, it can happen.

He has grown. Things are improving. He is paying his parking tickets.

We want the moon to begin with. Presidents, scholars and great athletes.

However, we'll take less. No, different. We want children who obey the law, sons and daughters who appreciate how much their mother loves them and people whose small victories we can revel in.

We don't want much. Not the moon, only 21-year-olds who we can love as much as we loved that 2-year-old who used to sit next to us with his thumb in his mouth while we read Goodnight Moon.

We don't want the moon, just a piece of their childhood sky and the kite we flew in the clouds.

"Thank you so much for dinner," he said the next day, not just in one, but in separate cell phone calls to both his mother and father. "I had a good time the rest of the night, but the best part was with you guys."

His parents didn't care if it was true. It sounded true and it was true for them.

In honor of his friends who didn't make it and the parents who were not lucky enough to sit across a table lit with candles and sparkling with wine glasses, we don't take this dinner for granted. We honor you, too. Herbie hasn't forgotten. Neither have his parents.

OLD TRUCK

I've got truck fever.

It's old truck fever, but new is probably just as bad. You want as much as wanting can be.

Ask yourself. Ask when you are rolling down the Grapevine, coming south from the Bay area, touching down at Meadows for the first time or leaving the maternity ward at Memorial.

Can you live in Bakersfield without a truck?

It has nothing to do with pay load, hauling capabilities and towability, although these are important. This is zen.

Have you noticed? The most relaxed people in the world are truck owners. Friends at work, my friend at Grimmway, my plumbing, wood-working, oil-pipe selling friends. They're at home in their own skins.

Is there anybody happier than an old guy in a truck? Old-guy trucks are some of the prettiest vehicles you'll ever see. Some of the most loved. Their owners drive around town with big smiles, and in this town, there are a million smiles.

Ask a man what the stupidest thing he ever did was, he'll tell you it was selling his truck. There is no percentage in selling a truck. No advantage unless you're buying another. No net gain unless you measure gain in terms of regret.

My mom gave me her green Mazda truck 15 years ago and I sold it a couple of years later. I still miss it. What did that truck do to me to warrant what I did to it?

How many times can you use a truck? If you live in an old neighborhood you can use it at least every weekend, but even new house people need them. Want to haul a bed, a piece of furniture, move a child out of or to college?

How often could you use a truck and have to borrow one from

a friend? They see you coming and they pity you. Their look says it all. "I have a truck, you don't." This conversation is over.

People try to pass Suburbans off as trucks because of the inside room. They're not trucks, they're trucks for people who want to take samba lessons and go out to dinner.

Trucks have beds. Open spaces you can throw things in, not a covered place in which to wrestle a mattress. In a truck, the sky is the ceiling and you own all the real estate in between.

There are two kinds of truck owners and I met one of them the other day at the cleaners. He was driving a brand new yellow truck. This truck was sweet as only a yellow truck can be and its owner was a young man, the son of a girl I had a crush on in high school.

He was a member of the "I don't haul anything in the back of my truck" club. It was too nice. You wouldn't risk the paint. He had it for other reasons that had nothing to do with the cubic feet of the bed.

Truck purists occupy the other camp. They don't care what the paint job looks like. A bad paint job is not only a badge of honor, but makes sense because then they don't have to worry about scratching it.

You can buy their truck. Yes, you can. When they die and their widow sells it, if there isn't a "do not sell" clause in his will.

If you buy a truck from a purist, know one thing. It won't be a small truck. Nor will it be a truck with "Luv" in the name.

Last Friday, I bought a white 1992 Chevy truck with 220,000 miles on it. Eighty bucks for five years. I can do that.

Tuesday, I took my first trip to the green waste facility off Mount Vernon with a truck full of leaves, lemon branches and pine wood. Along with the bike trail, the green waste facility is a good reason to live here.

I could have been dreaming, but I think the guys at the gate paid me more respect this time. I backed in next to a guy in a tan truck who was disgorging crate wood.

We noted each other's respective vehicles, nodded and continued with our business.

That was enough. Any more than that was just talk.

DAD'S 80TH

At least once, during the planning of your father's 80th birthday party, you will want to kill your whole family.

Dad is turning 80 in June. That's old and it isn't old. Some people look good for 80, others don't and a few are dead.

Dad looks good. He has fall color in his cheeks; he can still hike, ski, play tennis and try to save the Eastern Sierra in his spare time. He can laugh at himself and laugh harder at his children.

His only bad quality is that he and my mom raised six kids with opinions. Those kids married people who had opinions. The old man has a few himself.

Opinions are fine until you try to plan an 80th birthday party. Then you realize the world has too many opinions. Most of the opinions don't like each other.

We wanted to throw a party. That seemed like the right thing to do. Eat, visit, and listen to music. What could be simpler?

We decided to have the party at my sister's house in the East Bay. She offered. We accepted. Most of the family lives in the Bay Area and to get them to come to Bakersfield takes a subpoena.

There are only two things to disagree about when it comes to having a party: food and the guest list. The color of the tablecloths sailed through.

"I think Dad would like deviled eggs at his party," I said. "It's comfort food, and he should be comfortable with the food at his 80th birthday party."

There was silence on the other end of the line. I know what they were thinking. Deviled eggs. You've been on the farm too long.

Farm? That's what happens when you move to Northern California. All of a sudden you're too snooty for deviled eggs. I suppose the next thing you're going to be telling me is that you don't like Vienna sausages either.

Who doesn't like deviled eggs? Mustard, mayonnaise and some sweet pickle relish whipped into a feathery lightness and dusted with paprika. Served on a glass plate with egg indentations.

Have you ever noticed? The deviled eggs go first at a party. In a foot race with the shrimp, the eggs win. OK, no deviled eggs. Not fancy enough for the caterer. I can understand. The best deviled eggs come from humble kitchens with yellow tile countertops made by women who are at peace with skipping a workout or two at 24 Hour Fitness.

The next thing you're going to tell me is you want to have a salmon. Cold salmon. A large dead fish on the table.

There are people who think the world's problems can be solved if we just eat more salmon. I like salmon but I liked it better when we only had it once a year at the clambake. When there was less, I liked it more.

Salmon. When you get to be 80, it's time to celebrate. Take up smoking. Spread Cool Whip on your grapefruit.

My idea was flank steak. Who isn't happy when they see a big platter of flank steak? Meat calls to us. It sings lullabies to our bones.

If the menu doesn't inflame the troops, the guest list will. You can't invite everybody. If you did, they might come, eat the deviled eggs and you might have to talk to them.

Talking is work. No one wants to work at a party. You want good food, you want to trade superficialities, you want to sit down and rest your bones and when you're ready for dessert, you don't want anybody in your way.

Friends are like clothes. If you haven't worn them in a year, it's time to lighten the closet.

The guest list grew and it shrunk. People were voted off the island and then drifted back on. Reputations were savaged and subsequently rehabilitated with comments like, "Well, at least they won't require much attention."

By the time we were done with the heavy negotiation, the family was exhausted and unsure whether they ever wanted to see each other again.

We don't need a party, we need a mediation. We need the healing powers of a full plate of deviled eggs.

TEDDY

We celebrated by taking a walk. Teddy would have approved. If he could have, he would have been waiting at the back gate swinging his springer ears like a boxer before a fight.

Dogs don't want much. Expect much. Hope for much.

A bowl of food, a scrap of toast from the table if they can get it, a pat on the head, a romp in the river bed.

We could learn something. We probably have. Dogs bring out the best in us if we let them.

Two springers in one week. First my parents and now Teddy. Maybe they're somewhere where they can run together and please future masters like they have pleased us.

Teddy came through the classifieds. His mother died after

childbirth and his owner was bottle-feeding the puppies. He was happy to find them homes and quit the midnight feedings.

Although I promised Sue I would not talk about money, Teddy was free at the beginning and pretty free at the end. Along with the stellar qualities most dogs naturally exhibit, free isn't bad either.

Teddy alarmed us at first. One day, we looked in the backyard to see Teddy carrying Callie, our new kitten, in his mouth. It appeared that Teddy was having a snack.

He wasn't. The cat brought forth mothering instincts in him. He'd carry her around the yard, set her gently down and lick her.

A few years later, Teddy got hit by a car on 19th street while following me to Franklin School. He survived, retired from running for two years and then unretired, surprising the non-believers in the neighborhood.

A week ago, Teddy stopped at the gate before our morning walk. No more, he seemed to say. You go.

Monday, Thomas called. Teddy couldn't get up and was barking wildly. I came home to find him in the garage lying on the soft, white quilt breathing hard. Seizure, stroke, who knows. He couldn't get up, not even after his owners begged him to.

Eric, the vet, was wonderful.

So was the staff. So were the two women in the waiting room, who immediately understood when we walked in carrying Teddy wrapped in a sheet.

The vet calmly explained the options. He gave us time to talk about it. He left the room so we could say goodbye.

The vet couldn't have been better. I want him to give me the shot when it's my time to go. I'll try to be brave, too.

You wouldn't think going to the vet to put a dog down would qualify as a family outing, but if your son or daughter is at the right age, it can be. We huddled close in exam room No. 1.

Even when you're ready and it's the right thing, it's hard. Before the vet gave Teddy the shot, I unclipped his blue collar that was matted with brown hair. The collar sits on my desk. If you pick it up and close your eyes, you can smell the puppy.

He died with his head between his paws.

"He's so peaceful," Thomas said.

We say our goodbyes in a myriad of ways. I said mine this morning before the sun came up in a walk by the river. Gennie, the young black mutt, looked back.

Teddy was always trailing, and it was as if she was saying, "Where are you, my friend?"

To paraphrase a poet, I can see Teddy sniffing at every mole hole, at the base of every cottonwood tree and know whether I did or not he will have an honored place in the hearts of the small band that knew him.

Sam, I'm sorry, we couldn't have waited for you to come home.

HOT SAUCE

Anthony "Hot Sauce" Castillo is the 15th man on the Shafter High basketball team. The team is not having a great year, having won two games and lost 19.

The one bright spot is Sauce, as he is called by his teammates, an 18-year-old senior who is mildly retarded, has coordination problems and is a special education student at Shafter. Sauce is also the team's secret weapon. He fills seats, brings the crowd to its feet and soothes the sting of defeat.

Although the Generals possess unusual quickness and are sometimes competitive in the first half, more often than not, their game begins to unravel in the second half and by the time the fourth quarter dawns, the team often finds the game slipping away by double digit margins.

No one likes to lose. Getting hammered can be worse. The Generals are losing and getting hammered.

Enter Jeff Scott, the Shafter coach. Scott is the antidote to the sometimes charmless world of organized sports. Sure, Scott would like to win, but other things are important, too, he thinks. Those include participation, sportsmanship and compassion. That's where Sauce comes in.

The story started a few weeks ago with Shafter getting throttled by Garces. The Generals were down by 25 with three minutes to go when Scott called a timeout. He wanted to make a substitution because, as a good coach knows, sometimes putting in the right player can turn a game around.

Blowouts like this can be ugly. One team feels good about itself and the other rotten. Soon embarrassment turns to hurt and hurt becomes anger. The unrest on the floor can often spread to the stands making the atmosphere toxic.

After calling a timeout, Scott approached the two refs and told them he was putting in No. 50. "He's a special kid," he told them. "Can you keep an eye on him?

"I told the refs to tell Gino (Lacava, the Garces coach) what I was doing," Scott said. "It was up to Gino to do what he wanted."

No. 50 was the 5-foot-11-inch "Hot Sauce," so named because of his affinity for a player in a video game. Castillo, who keeps old sports sections in his dresser until they stack up and his mother throws them out, wanted to try out for basketball in November, and Scott, a special education teacher, encouraged him.

"He comes to practice every day," said his coach. "He participates in as many drills as he can. When he can't do the drill, he pulls himself out so his teammates can continue. He's been a blessing to our team."

That evening a few weeks ago, Castillo checked in with the scorer's table and went into the Garces game. He did what Coach Scott hoped he would do. He turned the game around.

Lacava understood immediately, counseling his players. Lacava, one of the most successful coaches in Kern County, did not get there without being a master strategist. No. 50 would require some special attention.

Both teammates and opposing players told him where to stand. Sauce found a wide-open path to the basket for three straight layups.

"That's my brother," yelled 17-year-old Robert Castillo from the stands.

Feeling his oats, Sauce tried and missed a three-pointer and then missed two free throws. Then he stripped a Garces player of the ball. By game's end, Sauce had scored six points and Shafter had lost 65-45.

"I've played a lot of basketball in my time, but that was the best three minutes of my life," Scott said. "The gym was rocking. Everybody was yelling for Anthony. I have new respect for Gino and his players."

Castillo's adoptive parents, Joe and Sally Arismendez, were

ecstatic. They shook the coach's hand until Scott, who has five children of his own, thought his hand was going to be separated from his arm.

"You made his life," the Arismendezes said, in only a slight overstatement.

Shafter has continued to lose. A few days ago, the team lost by 53 to Tehachapi. Scott, who left a gardening and landscape business to go back to school and become a teacher at age 47, is at peace with it. The players practice hard and Sauce keeps smiling.

Tuesday, Shafter played Garces again at Garces. Castillo's parents were in the audience along with his sister, brother-in-law, three second cousins and his brother Robert. Both Robert and Anthony were adopted by the Arismendezes 16 years ago when their niece, the boys' mother, began to have drug problems.

Robert is a whiz kid who will probably attend a major university. Next year, the Arismendezes have Anthony enrolled in a two-year program at Taft College and hope one day he will be self-sufficient.

Before Tuesday's game, Robert had to loan his brother his size-13 shoes because Anthony's were stolen the day before from his locker. He doesn't fully understand how the lockers work.

This Tuesday's game was different from the first one with Shafter putting up a ferocious fight. Layups followed steals and by halftime the score was 33-23, but it was a close 33-23. Shafter fans whispered this was the best game they'd seen the team play this year.

With 1:57 left, Garces led 66-55, and with 19.7 seconds to go, the lead had shrunk to seven. Scott looked up at the clock, looked down at the bench and seemed conflicted. He paced backwards. Scott had made a decision. It was Hot Sauce time.

With five seconds to go, Sauce got the ball under the basket. He shot and missed. He shot again and missed. With less than a second, zeroes starting to show on the clock, Sauce took one more shot. It bounced in. Garces won 69-63.

The crowd went wild. The mood inside the gym was close to the line from the Elton John song as in, "High as a kite by then."

"My wife cried," Garces fan Roark Randolph wrote in an e-mail.

"Heck, I even teared up."

After the game, the Shafter team mobbed their favorite teammate and then went to the locker room to change into blazers and ties.

"It's not cool to get beat, but he gets our hopes up," said teammate Juan Zavala.

BOB RUTLEDGE

Bob Rutledge can either sell you a small cricket cage, a carton of wax worms, a U-boat, a pole made by G. Loomis, a mess of garlic salted shad, a handful of lug worms from Korea, a jar of catfish cheese dip, or he can cook you cod poached in paper surrounded by herbs and served with wild rice and grilled tomatoes.

Your choice. He can do both.

Rutledge is a renaissance man who doesn't look like one. He's gruff, his eyes are deep set, his skin weathered, and he looks like he stayed up all night no matter how many hours of sleep he got. He owns Bob's Bait Bucket on South Chester and Kern River Bait on Niles.

He sells bait all day long. From 6 a.m. until 7 p.m., the shop has a steady stream of customers who always seem to be in a good mood. This is no surprise. They are going fishing. Customers either have the day off and are going fishing or are playing hooky and going fishing. Neither is bad.

The paper-cooked cod is another side of Rutledge, who grew up in Arvin and met his wife of 46 years when she was 12 and he was 15. His parents were part of "The Grapes of Wrath" migration from Arkansas in 1935. Past history includes working in a dairy, painting houses for 10 years and then opening the bait store 27 years ago.

Rutledge could always cook, but recently he learned how to cook better. A couple weeks ago, Rutledge graduated from Bakersfield College with a degree in culinary science.

The man is not in a hurry. It took him 10 years to get the degree. Rutledge squeezed in classes between the demands of running a store, being a husband, a father to three boys and one girl (the boys are in the bait business) a grandfather and a citizen of the world.

"My last class was algebra," Rutledge said. "That kicked my butt. I was lucky to get a C."

Going back to school started with his son, Ben, who 10 years ago wanted to open a restaurant.

"Let's go to school and learn something about food," his father suggested, and he did more than suggest it because it was Rutledge's money that was being called on to fund the restaurant.

Back to school they went and after a couple years Ben was pulled toward police work and Rutledge kept taking classes. Food sanitation classes, food purchasing classes, cooking classes and horticulture classes.

"I'm curious," he said. "Learning something new is one of the great things about being alive."

Rutledge fit school into his routine at the store, sometimes doing his homework in the back room. He still opens the south Chester shop seven days a week at 6 a.m. The day starts with Rutledge pouring himself a cup of coffee as black as night crawler bedding and grabbing 20-pound bar bells and doing 400 curls in sets of 10.

"If a customer comes in and isn't in a hurry, I'll finish the set," said the 68-year-old Rutledge. "If they are, I ring them up and get back to it later."

He calls his customers by name. They trade fishing stories. Some of them are even true.

By 9 a.m., exercise completed, paper read and register opened, and he goes home to visit with his wife, E.J. They sit in the garden and talk before she goes to work as a food server and trainer at Black Angus, something she has done for 29 years.

"I still love my wife," he said. "Her kisses taste as sweet as they did when she was 16."

Rutledge likes almost everything with the exception of the geese at Truxtun Lake that stop traffic. He thinks they ought to be captured and transported to Hart Park or Lake Ming.

That's about as dark as he gets. Rutledge welcomes change and progress. Take his neighborhood two blocks from the store that he is so fond of. It is now filled with a rich, ethnic stew that includes Guatemalans, Vietnamese, Hispanics and blacks.

Rutledge is a learner and a reader. Presently he's reading The Power of Myth by Joseph Campbell. In the fall, he'd like to continue his education with a history course and a class in psychology.

This wasn't his first shot at college. Rutledge started BC in 1955 but had to quit because his father fell out of a haystack and broke his leg. Rutledge took his place in the dairy and didn't go back to school until 10 years ago.

The wait was worth it. He'd wrapped fish in paper, but never cooked in it. Now he's done both.

THE WEST WING

When the show ended and the camera panned the White House, I looked over to see if there were tears.

It was dark, but I think the reflection of Jed Bartlett glistened in her eyes.

We are in mourning. One day, we'll open the curtains again. Receive visitors. Wear colors.

Last Sunday, *The West Wing* ended. We lost the only Democratic president who could actually make millions of Republicans forgive party affiliation for an hour each week.

(Thank goodness Josh finally came to his senses and found love. C.J. Cregg, too. I was glad to see Sam Seaborn return and Toby get pardoned.)

Sunday was Mother's Day, and it was only because it was Mother's Day that we tivoed *The West Wing*.

If it had been a normal Sunday night with dinner guests, it would have been understood that either the evening ended at 8 p.m., West Wing time, or that the guests would retire to our oval office to watch the show.

Our grown children knew that calling their mother between 8 and 9 p.m. on Sunday meant either having the phone call go straight to the answering machine or having the conversation cut short.

We grow attached to our TV shows. They become part of our weekly rituals and give purpose to an otherwise quiet evening.

As couples, it gives us something to talk about before we go to sleep. At breakfast. A good TV show can add years to a relationship.

When you ran out of conversation, there was always the presidential race or the romantic tension between Josh and Donna on *The West Wing*.

What now? Am I going to have to talk about my day? Do we look for another program and, if so, what is the appropriate period of mourning before we choose one?

Good TV shows are like dogs. When you lose a good dog, you don't toss his dish out right away. Nor do you immediately go to the pound. When you are ready for a new dog, it's better if the dog finds you as much as you find the dog. I suspect this may hold true for TV, too.

I haven't seen any of the reality shows, the talent shows or the new comedies. Why do we need another comedy when we can still watch *Seinfeld* reruns?

Every new show gets compared to the great ones before it. Often, the new one pales. It may have less to do with the quality of the shows and everything with my being a crabby fiftysomething.

This is what I'll miss about West Wing: Jed Bartlett. He's an argument for three-term presidents. The snappy dialogue, the breakneck pace, the humor that comes with exhaustion and characters who took themselves much too seriously but knew it was great theater anyway.

Most of all, I'll miss Sunday nights, the dark room and the dishes that had to wait. This is one way to spend time together.

Hail to the chief.

FATHER AND SON DOUBLES

I recently entered the Kern County Open Doubles Championship with my 16-year-old son.

What better way to spend time with a son or daughter than sharing a tennis court with them. It is an activity that requires teamwork, cooperation, and is enjoyable besides.

Does it get any better?

Yes, it does when you consider the opportunity to teach your child something about the world. Sports are not only a paradigm for life but when you have a parent who is expert at something like tennis, the child can improve almost by osmosis.

In the first round, we drew two 40-ish players who play at the Stockdale Country Club. What I knew about them was they were decent players and they were tall.

"Thomas, if we get our first serves in and make a couple of returns, we'll be fine," I said.

That's what I said, but what I was thinking was, "These guys have no idea what they're getting into. If you laid all the tall guys I've beaten head to head, you could go around the earth twice. Tall guys are on my payroll.

The warm-up was friendly. I like to keep it friendly. It's better that way so when you win, your opponents don't think you are gloating.

We lost the first point. Thomas served and I crossed in to cut off the return, but dumped it in the bottom of the net. No worry. I made a statement: I could and would rule the net like Magellan ruled the seas.

We lost the second game. That's OK, we're only down a break and it was my serve. Watch out, the fire was about to come down from the mountain.

I hit three volleys, each slower than the one before it. They looked like big yellow butterflies.

Before I knew it, we had lost the first set 6-0.

"Thomas, this is where we dig in, where we plant our flag," I say. "This is where we turn the match around."

I served to lead off the second set. That's the way I liked it. I'm the father; I showed leadership. I hit two 5 mph serves and then two slower than that. In case you don't know how fast that is, imagine throwing a cotton ball underhanded against a fan.

The enemy held the serve. Thomas, who was giving it everything he had, lost his serve. I had a sitter at the net that I nearly whiffed. It was 6-0, 3-0. I was sweating like a meth addict. We approached uh-oh time.

"Uh-oh time" was when the aggrieved party, in this case us, wondered if they were capable of winning a game.

The specter of being beaten 6-0, 6-0 hung over us like smoke over a campfire. There was no athletic equivalent to being beaten 0 and 0. What it suggested was not only should you consider abandoning the sport, but a change in ZIP code might be appropriate too.

At 6-0, 3-0, Thomas' mother left. Other friends who had stopped to watch backpedaled. This was not just a massacre, it could be a virus. No one wanted to catch what we had.

Six-0, 5-0. The match had become a blur. We lost points in great clumps like a man losing his hair. Soon he will be bald and we will be finished.

Our opponents were in somewhat of a quandary. Do they give us a game or do they put us out of our misery? Pity wafted across the net like stale perfume.

On match point, our ball flew long. We'd been double bageled. I shook Thomas' hand and congratulated our opponents. I wanted to kill everything within five miles, including the animals and the birds.

I walked off the court. People turned their heads and suddenly took an interest in the tops of their shoes.

Thomas learned something. I was not eager to ask what it might have been.

FREE JACUZZI

Somebody gave me a free hot tub. It didn't cost me a dime. Not one penny.

The Jacuzzi sits in my garage. It's big—6 ½ feet by 6 ½ feet. One day — soon! — I will move it to the back yard and hook it up.

A friend already has money on this beast never seeing daylight. And if it does see daylight, we'll use it twice, lose interest, have a big old white elephant in the back yard and then offer a "free" Jacuzzi to someone else.

Hot tubs elicit one of two reactions. People either shake their heads or nod enthusiastically. The head shakers have been there. They had one, went in it every day for a month, then the pump broke, summer came and they never lifted the cover again.

"I finally took mine out with a sledgehammer," said Russ.

The negative people are passionately negative. Not only do they think it was the dumbest thing they ever did, but since they're telling you how dumb it was and you don't get the message makes you double dumb.

Then, there are the people whose lives hot tubs have saved. Hot tubs that saved their backs, their knees and their marriages. They speak of Jacuzzis in the same manner as those people who love Hawaii.

Given the abundance of lightly used hot tubs, it is not necessary to buy one. Merely put out the word in the discarded Jacuzzi network. Real-estate agents know where all the hot tubs have gone to die.

I told Mike. Within six months, he had located four. Three of the parties wanted money. The fourth wanted theirs gone. The free one belonged to his parents.

"Did you think about starting it first?" asked hot-tub pessimist Russ.

Jacuzzis are heavy. No matter how many people you think you're going to need, add two. Then bring your father and every male child over 12. We had seven people and even with seven, it was barely enough.

"Call me when your hot tub is hooked up, steam is rising off the water, the wine is open and you've already poured me a glass," Russ said, when I told him I was trolling for volunteers.

Free is a relative term. Especially with the hot tub we dragged down from the backside of Bear Mountain.

Free didn't include the truck I rented from U-Haul for $126, plus $50 in gas. Nor did it cover the two men I hired for $60 each. No one has enough friends to move a hot tub. And if you do, you will have fewer when you are done.

"Free" didn't account for the Jacuzzi's massiveness. You can't just throw it in the backyard like a Doughboy. Free does not include the hole you probably have to dig, the cement you have to pour, the plants you have to plant around it with which to disguise it.

Then, there is the electrical. You can't "homemade" that one; otherwise you'll electrocute all of your children's friends the first time they have a bikini party in your Jacuzzi.

"Six People Electrocuted by Careless Jacuzzi Owner."

The hot tub sits in the garage. It's free as can be. Free of power, free of water and free of people.

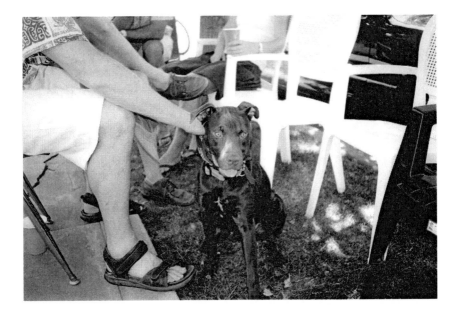

GOODBYE POLO

A friend brought a shovel. The hole was dug, but he helped me fill it in. That's a friend.

The dirt was moist, dark and easy to work. No roots. Maybe two or three, but they sliced apart with the sharp end of the shovel.

I buried him close to where the Jacuzzi is supposed to go on the side of the house. Under an orchid tree and next to the woodpile. If the Jacuzzi ever gets put in, I can sit there and think about what a sweet dog he was.

Polo was not ugly to me. Not the first time I saw him in the bushes near the picnic tables at Yokuts Park. Not when I laid him in the dark, soft dirt. If anything, in death the pit bull features seemed to soften.

The wrinkles had been made smooth. The drawn quality to his eyes had relaxed. The white bumps under his chin were gone. Maybe this is how he would look when he gets where he is going. A face that says, "Don't be afraid. You will love me like my old master did."

Even if his face hadn't changed a bit, where more of the chocolate Lab was present in him than the pit bull, it wouldn't have mattered to me.

I liked the pit bull in him. It was character. The severe features were a contrast to his personalty.

I've never been licked so much by a dog. In the morning, at the back door, at the gate, at noon or in the evening, that's how he'd greet me. Greet anybody.

Lick your hands, your legs, your face.

I know what you're thinking. Everybody thinks they have the sweetest dog in the world. Count me in. I'm just one more everybody.

Each of us can produce a thousand stories about what makes our dog the sweetest dog in the world. Friends listen, but they don't. Who can blame them? They have their own stories.

In the end, the only story that counts is the one between a dog and its master. That story is really not meant to travel. That narrative, added to daily with satisfying slices of ordinary life, is what makes it hard to say goodbye.

Wednesday morning, I came downstairs to fix Thomas breakfast and afterward to walk the dogs. When I had plenty of time, I took them to the river. When I didn't, it was Jastro Park. They didn't care—a romp was a romp.

I looked out the back window and the gate was open. The latch undone. Polo was gone.

We have a brown dog and a black dog. One of each. A team.

Usually, they stick together. Even if they get out. Not this time.

This time, Gennie, the black dog, was sitting on the deck. I went out the back gate and whistled. Nothing. Then I rode west on 20th Street.

I spotted him lying on the sidewalk, two blocks down. He was motionless. His eyes were open. There wasn't a drop of blood on him. He still smelled like a puppy.

I held him in my arms. You know how it is. You think things that are not possible. I thought if he could feel my heart beating his would too.

I loved him more every day. Have I said that already?

When we first brought Polo home, we had visited the vet.

"You have a good dog, but he has a heart murmur," Eric said.

I didn't think much of it, but after he ran across the park, he would stop and gasp, throwing his head back. Then he would take off and run again.

I hope it was his heart. Not a car. It seems better that way. I don't know why.

I wrapped him in a golden wool blanket that I kept in the garage. That blanket was familiar to him. I had spread it out on the concrete when I did sit-ups. Polo would put his head on my shoulder and nuzzle my ears.

Every day since the day he came home with me, he would wait for me in the garage with his back against the Jacuzzi. It was an odd sort of security pillow. He would look up to me as if to say, "When are you going to hook this thing up?"

I committed Polo and that ugly golden blanket to the rich, dark downtown soil. Someday, there will be a Jacuzzi next to his grave and he will be home again. I can only imagine sitting in the warm water and having that sweet, humble dog lick my ears.

After I buried him, I went inside and opened the fridge. On the third shelf was a plastic bag full of flank steak scraps I'd saved for the dogs.

I'd give anything to feed him one more time.

COLLECTOR'S CORNER

The last call to KNZR's *Collector's Corner*, the radio program where for almost 40 years you could buy, sell or swap, was from Teresa, who had a queen-sized headboard and two nightstands for sale.

The call sheet kept by the show's host, the radio smooth Don Howard, indicates Geri had a cement mixer he wanted to move, Elena was looking for a flute, Tim was selling four old Chevy motors and Yolanda had a pot-bellied pig named Chiquita she was trying to place in a nice home, but "no sausages please."

Folks talking to folks.

That's what *Collector's Corner* was.

It wasn't folks yelling at folks, folks insulting folks or folks giving advice to folks.

Just folks talking to folks.

On March 1, *Collector's Corner*, officially died, but it had been losing steam for years. The show, described by listeners as an episode of Sanford and Son, an on-air flea market, an extended party line, a continuous garage sale and newspaper without ink on your hands, had moved from Monday through Friday 8 a.m. to noon, to Saturdays at 5:30 a.m.

What finally killed *Collector's Corner* was not only eBay, Sunday swap meets, liquidation sales, the shopping channel, the 99 cent stores, but a world that had shifted gears from second to fourth and then blasted into overdrive.

Who had four hours to listen to the program whose slow pace, rural flavor and voices suggesting Oklahoma, Texas, Missouri, and Arkansas were as much a part of the charm as the goods being peddled?

Who had four hours to do anything other than chase around? Jump in and out of cars? Not enough listeners to convince longtime advertisers like BS&W ("All over town, they're living proof, you can't top a Bakersfield Shingles Wholesale roof") to continue paying $150 an hour to keep it on the air.

Collector's Corner was the brain child of former radio men Dan Speare and Dexter Haymond who started the show on KGEE (and later moved it to KPMC) in 1965, after visiting Las Vegas and listening to a similar version called The Trading Post.

"In the beginning, we played old standards — music from the '40s and '50s — along with the phone calls," said Speare, who sold KPMC in January 1990. "Finally, we got more phone calls than we could handle and we eliminated the music."

Although the idea (called "tradio" — a show that features selling, buying and trading) had immediate carry, before advertisers would sell it out, the show needed and found a host in George Gholston.

Gholston was a former truck driver who had lost his left arm in an accident. He wore gold rings on the fingers of his prosthetic hand. He was also black, something unbeknownst to many of his white listeners at the beginning.

Gholston had a rich tenor voice honed by singing in the Bakersfield Singers Association.

He came to work every day dressed in a dark suit because he doubled as a salesman for *Collector's Corner*.

"The first sales appointment he had was with Sullivan's, the ladies clothing store in Oildale on North Chester and he brought back a contract (a commitment to advertise)," said Speare.

"We got a call from the owner who said, 'Who is this black man you sent into Oildale?' There was a pause. 'He's the nicest gentleman we've ever had and we hope he will call on us in the future.'"

Advertisers were sometimes tricky and required deft handling.

"Once Sandstone Brick Co. had a toilet they were selling," Speare said. "In order to introduce it, we played the sound of a toilet flushing in the background. Bill Heisey (one of the owners) called and he was really frosted. 'How can you do this to our image?'

"Thirty minutes he called back to apologize and said that people were calling and that they had never gotten a response like this."

Collector's Corner, Speare said, turned out to be the most successful show he'd ever had. Although Speare did not know it at the time, Collector's Corner, laid the groundwork for talk radio and the flood of call-in shows that were to follow.

However, it was talk radio the old-fashioned way. Neighbor to neighbor. The show was a way of getting acquainted with people or catching up with those you'd lost contact with.

"You knew somebody's mom had died when they cleaned out her garage and were selling her refrigerator," said Rogers Brandon, a local radio station owner.

Gholston, who died in 1990 of a heart attack, would usually close his show the same way.

"If you have an appointment at a quarter to 12, slow down because you've got a long way to go and a short time to get there."

Slow down. Now or then, advice worth collecting.

SAM AND A SECOND CHANCE

The Friday morning before Thanksgiving, our 20-year-old son, Sam, was in an automobile accident in San Diego. Life is a game of inches and, Friday, every inch counted. In his greatest hour of need, he had his greatest stroke of luck. He ran into a telephone pole or a light stanchion with his Chevy Tahoe, a beast of a vehicle, but he was wearing his seatbelt and his airbags deployed.

I used to think that nothing good happened late at night. After midnight. Early in the morning.

Then I remembered, that's not true. Good happens too. Children are born then. Two of ours were.

However, parents dread the phone call after midnight. No one is calling to inform you that you have won the lottery. Usually, the news is not good, and sometimes it's worse than that.

I'd gotten up at 5:30. a.m. There were two 858 numbers on my cell phone screen. Eight-five-eight. Where was that?

Then I remembered. San Diego. Sam lives there.

This was the voice mail:

"Hi, I am Benny from Sharp Memorial Hospital in San Diego. We are looking for the parents of Samuel John Benham. He is in the ICU."

We were in the car in 15 minutes. I've never seen Sam's mother pack so quickly.

There are silent moments between a husband and a wife. It's not as if there is nothing to say; there is plenty. There is plenty to say, but no one dares say it.

I always thought I was Mr. Cool. The go-to guy in emergency situations. I've been giving myself more credit than I deserve and, Sam's mother, less than she is due.

I was a mess. Sue was calm. I couldn't get through a cell phone call. Sue plowed through one after another.

I started to make deals with the Divine. You always do. I'll be good from now on, I won't squander any more money on the Jacuzzi project, I won't buy the new bike I want. Take it all, but let that tow-headed, independent, drive-his-mother-crazy boy live.

What you think about when your children graduate from high school, get married or are lying in a hospital bed sedated and hooked up to a breathing machine is not the man or woman they have become, but the boy or girl they once were.

When Sam was 2, I wrote: "When I come home at night, he is the first one to greet me. He puts his arms up in the air to be hugged. His face is all ridges, folds and smiles.

"He is like a little planet, suspended there, vibrating with happiness. His face is full of light. It's wonderful."

That's what you think about when you are waiting to hear the answers about head injuries, spinal cord injuries or just making it through. Our children do not know, and I'm not sure they can, how much we have invested in them. I'm not talking about money. They are looking forward, we are looking back.

I learned a couple of things on the ride down to San Diego.

We don't need newspapers. Or radio. TV either.

When something serious happens, it gets around town in minutes. The human network is much faster than the commercial one.

I also learned what friends have been telling me for years. When it's your turn in what Jon Stewart calls the seat of heat, people will be sitting next to you. The auditorium may be dark, but it will be filled.

However, the journey starts alone. Or almost alone. Tragedy, or in this case, near tragedy, is not inclusive.

Is it always like this? A beautiful clear day once the sun comes out. Eighty degrees, perfect beach weather. Heaven and a hospital bed.

By LAX, we'd spoken to Fran, Sam's ICU nurse. Thank God for nurses.

"He is stable. We have him sedated, because we want to run a CT scan. I think he is going to be all right."

It was good news, but no one believes it. Not completely. Until you're sitting there holding his hand and looking into his blue eyes, you don't believe anything.

The traffic parted past LAX and stayed parted through Orange County. We arrived at the hospital by 10:30 a.m. We were in the ICU and at bed No. 16, Sam's bed, by 10:45. Time seems more important in these situations. It's something to hang on to.

ICU is like theater in the round. There is drama everywhere. Everybody is visible.

If you have ever seen somebody in a casket, their faces seem smaller. As if they have shrunk.

In the ICU, at least for Sam, his face seemed larger. I'm not sure it meant anything. I just noticed it.

"We're going to wait until 12 to bring him out and ask him some questions," Fran said.

"We'll ask him to follow some simple commands. If he is unable to follow them, we'll put him under again."

Noon came, his breathing tube was removed and the anesthesia shut off. Sam came to almost instantly. His face had that ICU combination of terror and confusion.

"Sam, you've had a bad accident and you are in the hospital," Fran said. "Your parents are here. You are going to be OK."

Fran asked him to wiggle his toes. Toes were wiggled. She asked him to hold up two fingers and Sam held up his whole hand.

"Two fingers, Sam," she said.

He held up three fingers and the nurse shook her head. Hey, wait a second. Sam's parents were liberal arts majors. In our book, three is pretty close to two.

I knew Sam was going to be OK when, about the third thing he said before, "Hi, Mom and Dad," was, "Where's my wallet?"

Sam likes to know where his wallet is. He knows exactly what is in his wallet, and he wanted to make sure what was in it, was still in it.

Sam left the hospital six hours later with his parents. He came home to Bakersfield. Healing has included Greek lemon chicken soup.

At dinner the other night, Thomas, Sam's younger brother, said, "Sam may have used up all of the luck in this family. I'd better be careful."

Yes, be careful. You and the rest of your posse.

CARRIE MAE HILL

Carrie Mae Hill cleaned houses so her children didn't have to. She cleaned houses so her children didn't have to unless those houses were their own.

Moreover, she did it with pride and elevated it to something akin to art.

Her obituary was in Wednesday's paper. Seventy-nine years old. Mother of six children, one stillborn. Married for 48 years. Husband died in 1984.

Clues were scattered through the obituary like crumbs in the forest. She was "highly skilled in her lifelong career as a domestic worker." She "returned to school following retirement." At the end was, "In lieu of flowers, please send donations to the Kern Adult Literacy Council."

This is one of those "where do you start?" stories. You can start at the beginning or you can start at the end. The middle isn't bad either.

Nine years ago, Hill, walked into the Kern Adult Literacy Council on 18th Street. She was 70. She wanted to learn how to read and write.

"She had two goals," said her tutor, Patricia Archer. "She wanted to be able to read her Bible and she wanted to be able to send out Christmas cards."

No one knew. Not her family. Not her friends. Not her employers. Hill had a powerful memory that crunched phone numbers, directions and lists with an exactness that led people to think she read and wrote fluently. She completed the illusion by speaking as if she had graduated from Oxford.

For years at Mount Zion Missionary Baptist Church, Hill had

seen her fellow parishioners move their fingers across their hymnals and Bibles as they sang and recited. She did the same, moving her finger across the page so that no one would know she was doing it by memory.

Despite her lack of formal training, or maybe because of it, Hill pushed education with her children. School was an automatic. College a given.

"With my grandmother, it was never, 'Are you going to college?'" said her grandson, local attorney Curtis Floyd. "It was, 'Where are you going to college?'"

When the family celebrated college graduations, advanced degrees and prestigious jobs, Hill was happy but matter of fact.

"It was as if she was saying, you knew you could do that," Floyd said.

The results were impressive. Two of her children earned Ph.D's, two of her grandchildren have been to law school and one to engineering school. The Hill tribe, and she preferred the American Indian version of the word "tribe" because it meant "no one was left behind" also includes an FBI agent, a caterer, a teacher, a transit worker, a middle school principal and a college educator.

"You look at a lot of people who are born on third base and never make it home," said orthopedic surgeon Mike Tivnon, who performed several hip surgeries on Hill. "Her children had none of the advantages, but they all crossed the plate."

Not bad for a mother who couldn't read or write until she was 70.

Not bad for someone who was born in Beggs, Okla., for someone who was married at 11 and stayed married to the same man for 48 years.

Not bad for someone who had her first child before she was 13, worked in the fields picking cotton and peas and lived part of her married life in a tent with a dirt floor beside a ditch.

"She would would sweep the floors for 30 minutes a day until there was no dust left and the dirt was hardened," Floyd said. "We were poor, but Yai-Yai (Greek for grandmother) was going to have a clean house."

A clean house. That was Hill's trademark both in her work as a domestic and at home.

"The second house we lived in was almost a shack but it was immaculate," said her son, Willis Jr. "Children could not go into the living room unless you were dressed to go to church or dressed to go to town. You'd look at the outside of the house and you wondered why you couldn't go in there."

The toilet at that house was outside. Willis remembers his mother putting linoleum on the floor, plastering linoleum on the walls and then constantly washing it with disinfectant. If somebody were to come to her house, she wanted her toilet to be clean even if it was an outhouse.

"I hate to say that she even worked for us because she was like a mother to me and a grandmother to my children," said Napier Hill, one of the four families Hill worked for over her 50-plus years as a domestic.

"She was so dignified, she had such perfect posture and marvelous carriage and she was always dressed as neat as a pin. Her standards were so high for both herself and the people around her that you'd almost pick things up before she arrived."

Hill, whose job recommendations started and finished with "you've got to hire this lady," was much more than a housekeeper. She was a great cook, a trusted confidante, a warm influence on the children she took care of and a woman who stayed fast with her families from birth to death.

"When my mother died in 1997 she came by for the wake," said Al Sandrini, a family Hill worked for for more than 30 years.

"We wanted her there as a guest. Mrs. Hill insisted on working, preparing food, serving it and she even cleaned up at the end. She was not to be stopped."

One of her early jobs was working for Don Clark, the caterer, with whom she started when he opened his business. By then Hill, had lost her son Curtis Hill, a great wide receiver who died in the plane crash on Oct. 29, 1960, that claimed 22 people including 17 members of the Cal Poly football team.

"I lost my son when he was 18 and she showed up after the

funeral and starting working in the kitchen," Clark said. "She poured coffee and made food."

At her own funeral Thursday at the Mount Zion Missionary Baptist Church, more than one person referred to Hill as "that great soldier you have loaned us."

Truth told she was more a general than a soldier. She ran the house, and no one, not even her husband, Willis Sr., who spent most of his whole life working at Kern Valley Packing, disagreed.

While Willis senior worked in the shipyards up north during World War II, Hill stayed behind with the four children. Every two weeks, Willis sent his check to his wife in Bakersfield.

"When he moved back to Bakersfield, she told him they were buying a house," Willis Jr. said.

"How can we buy a house?" he said. She had saved every dime he sent her and added to it.

She was careful about what she bought and shopped for quality. She had antique furniture which she took meticulous care of. She also had a rust-colored suede jacket which she prized.

"I remember going to visit her sister and brother who lived with her grandparents in Corcoran," said her son Willis Jr. "Her brother had an affection for her suede jacket and so she gave it to him. She didn't have that many jackets in her closet but she was willing to do that for her brother."

In 1994, her work done with the families she had taken care of and her own family grown and prospering, Hill began learning how to read and write.

By then she had moved to southwest Bakersfield and had become an avid walker. When she took her walks along Stockdale Highway, she studied the vowels she had written on the palm of her hand.

At her funeral, her grandson Todd said that "in her educational awakening, our system of letters and words were no longer just shapes and symbols, but names, people and voices."

The more she learned, the greater her appetite grew for dates, for historical events and for facts.

"One day, she went to the fair and she called me and she was so excited," said Archer, her tutor, who became a close friend. "I can read the signs on the doors, the rides and the exhibits. God bless you."

Reading also meant she could go dinner parties at her daughter Caren's sorority and fill out the dinner ticket so she would have a chance to win the door prize. It meant she could conduct business at the post office without being embarrassed.

Two years ago at the age of 77, Hill waltzed into the Kern Adult Literacy Office waving a white paper. Donna Hilton, the director, had no idea what the paper was or why she was so happy.

"I've passed my written driving test," Hill said proudly.

She had missed three questions. Hill had the test framed and hung it on her wall at home in her sitting room.

Learning to read also gave Hill a chance to reflect on her life. Archer remembers reading together and seeing Hill with her head bowed and tears streaming from her chestnut-colored eyes.

"Life would have been so different if I would have known how to read," Hill said. "I could have really helped my children."

Archer did what good teachers do when they hear a mistake. She corrected her.

"You have your family and you have love. That's what most people strive for."

BARBERSHOP ESCAPE

Fridays, every two weeks, are good because I can visit Charlie, the female barber who makes things right again.

Pleasure begins with driving up and seeing the spinning barber pole, an indication that the Westchester Barber Shop is open. The spinning pole quiets blood pressure like a cup of Sleepytime tea relaxes before bed.

Men are simple. That much we know. They are never more childlike than when they are standing in front of the spinning pole, looking through the glass and watching their favorite barber leisurely running her hands through another customer's hair.

Yes, simple. A friend sent me an e-mail with several attachments delineating the differences between men and women.

One had a picture of a single on-and-off switch -- obviously a man. The woman was illustrated by a photo that had an assortment of switches, buttons, lights and knobs.

Men are not looking for drama in their barbershop. There is enough drama outside the barbershop. Inside is a place of relative calm. It is is the quiet of eternity.

Which is to say not much changes. The pictures on the wall of barbershops dating to the 1800s, the western sayings etched on wood and the hunting and car magazines strewn on the cracked leather chairs.

No, not much changes, the least of which is the kind of haircut men ask for. That rarely varies. A man asks for the same haircut he had last time and that he had the time before last.

A haircut is not about forging a new path. It's a return to the familiar. A communion with the past that now, sitting in the red barber's chair, raised after being pumped up by hand, seems as close as the mirror behind your head.

I wouldn't call it dramatic tension, but a good haircut builds. It starts with the barber putting her hands on your shoulders, asking if you want the usual, running her hands through your hair as if assessing its health and length and then pirouetting gracefully toward the table underneath the mirror for the appropriate scissors or clippers.

This is all warm-up, however — barber foreplay -- because what a man has interrupted his day for is to have his collar unloosened, and at the end of the haircut, have his neck shaved. Heaven.

Most men will pay $15, plus a $2 tip, for that alone. Fifteen dollars for a loosening of the collar and the feel of the steel blade on the back of his neck.

Years ago, and maybe it still happens in some quarters, barbers would apply hot shaving cream and then scrape it off with a straight razor stropped on a piece of leather. That was the crescendo at the end of a beautiful symphony.

Charlie doesn't do that anymore. However, even with the electric clippers, the sensation is hypnotic. Please don't stop. Are you sure you got everything? A man quietly begs.

"Do you want me to shave your neck a little lower?" she asks, pulling down the shirt and revealing an inch or two of the upper back.

Yes, please do. And you might take a look at my shoulders too. That and the top of my feet.

After Charlie returns the clippers to the table, she cleans the neck area with a soft brush. That's your cue to run your hand over your smooth neck. Not once, but several times.

Now, you are ready to face the world again. Anything is possible with a newly shaved neck. Especially when a return to the barber is on the horizon.

PROM NIGHT

"They all look like a bunch of hookers."

This statement, uttered or thought by every adult within 20 square miles, can only mean one thing: it's prom time.

Don't spit out your Special K. I'm not saying that these generally well-mannered, high-spirited, college-bound girls are hookers, they just look like they could be in the lineup.

Last weekend, our 17-year-old son attended the prom. He had a date who, as per the present custom, was not a girl with whom he was romantically involved. She, as do many of them, looked like a movie star.

I never went to a prom in high school. Nor a formal. Back then, a girl had to like you to go on a date with you.

These days, if you can't get a date, you can always go with a buddy.

When I was 16, you didn't go with a buddy. Not at South High. There was nothing wrong with having buddies, it was just illegal to go on dates with them.

If you have high school-age children, you know the drill. The evening begins with pictures at the house of one of the attendees at around 4:45 p.m. For the girls and their mothers, the evening has started before dawn with nails, hair, flowers, the dress and a call to the World Bank in order to secure a loan.

No, the prom is not cheap.

The boys just show up. Boys are good at that. As long as their ties are the same orange color as their date's dress, showing up is all they need to do.

You can tell the girls who have the shortest dresses. Their fathers are doing tequila shooters at the photo op. Sometimes, they dispense with the glass and just empty the bottle.

A mother and daughter have learned one thing: Do not preview the prom dress for Dad. Show up at pictures with the dress on when it's too late to do anything about it and when there are too many other people around to say anything.

The only sensible response for a father, when he sees how short his daughter's dress is, is to place his head in a vise and turn the handle two times to the right. Only this will obliterate the image of his little girl dressed in something no bigger than a mouse pad.

Not having a daughter at this prom, I had planned to enjoy myself at the photo session. I headed for the kitchen counter replete with open bottles of wine and the cheese and salami combo plate. I was so hungry, I leaned quickly forward to take a Triscuit and a cube of cheddar and banged my head against the corner of an overhead cabinet.

Great. Now, I had a small, bleeding hole in the middle of my forehead that said, "I was hanging out by the cheese platter and making fun of the fathers who had daughters wearing short skirts."

It never pays to gloat. I have a moon shot in the middle of my forehead to prove it.

I dabbed my wound. It was still bleeding. I was probably going to need plastic surgery or a head transplant.

Later that evening, after the photos and the pre-prom dinner, where one of the moms had killed herself for two days making enough food for 12 couples and 24 parents, one of the boys had trouble getting into the prom because he was wearing the wrong colored tennis shoes.

That was his mistake. He should have gone in his underwear. No one would have noticed.

MOM'S 80TH

I've heard the song a million times. Who hasn't? But I've never heard "Try to Remember" quite the way my dad sang it to my mom on her 80th birthday last Sunday underneath the cottonwood trees at Rainbow Tarns near Mammoth Lakes.

Sure, my dad is a ham. A natural-born singer who used to thrill and terrify his kids with booming renditions of songs from Oklahoma!, Damn Yankees, and For the Love of Maggie.

This, however, wasn't about trying to hit the back wall at the Harvey Auditorium.

This was about singing a song as tenderly as you can for a woman you've lived with and loved for almost 60 years.

This was about payback, admiration and awe.

Yes, "awe." God, my mom is tough. I saw her pick up a rattlesnake once on a walk near Edison. The rattlesnake wasn't huge, but it wasn't dead, either. She put it in a paper bag. We took it home.

She skied Mammoth top to bottom in a sealskin coat when she was 65. Mercifully, she waited for us halfway down, looking back up the hill wondering where we were and why we were taking so long.

Eventually, we could out-hike her. About two years ago. Or maybe last week.

She hiked 10 miles in the Sierra when she was six months' pregnant with my oldest brother, Mark. No wonder he turned out like he did.

He was born with her physical craziness. The no-quit thing. No-quit when you should quit.

Our whole family gathered last weekend at Mammoth to

celebrate her birthday. We are six kids. We haven't always gotten along. Not getting along is one thing; your mother's 80th birthday is another.

Everybody made it. All six. Six kids plus spouses, grandchildren, sisters, nieces, nephews, even her cousin, Bob Sidenberg and his wife, Susan, from Minneapolis.

My parents can die now, something they don't plan to do, but if they do, they can die happy.

Mom's quirky. An original. I know everybody says that, but it fits her.

A couple of months ago, when I was visiting them at Mammoth, there was a speckled bird on the table inside the front door. It was a pretty bird, but a dead bird. My mom had taken a fancy to the bird on a walk and so home it came.

And home it was on the downstairs table for the next three days.

Imagine my brother, Courtney's surprise when he opened his freezer recently and found a dead egret. Mom, he thought. Mom, he was right.

Anna, my 13-year-old niece, was flying with her grandmother when a black bird with red markings ran into the window of the plane.

"That's a yellow bellied sap sucker or something," Mom said.

Courtney was also flying with her once—she's been a pilot since she was 14—when he accidentally knocked open the window with his elbow at 10,000 feet.

Courtney was in a panic, but she reached across him with her right hand and closed the window without missing a beat.

She was the president of Planned Parenthood in Bakersfield in the '60s and '70s. That was funny. Six kids, president of Planned Parenthood.

She taught at South High for a while. I run into girls, now women, who knew her. They all say the same thing. She taught, by example that it was OK to believe in yourself no matter how much evidence there was to the contrary.

She could train a dog, jump a horse and throw a pot. I never heard her say, "I can't do this, climb this, or finish this."

That makes an impression.

Cotton from the cottonwood trees floated through the party by the stream stocked with baby trout. The grandchildren laughed and played on two hammocks as the jazz combo fired up one more song.

Dad took the mike. He sang "What a Wonderful World."

My mom looked delighted. The rest of us dissolved. There is something about a guy singing his girl a love song.

I see skies of blue and clouds of white
The bright blessed day, the dark sacred night
And I think to myself, what a wonderful world.
Amen.

ALL CLEAR

The Lakers are struggling, my Jacuzzi smells like a swamp and now I can't eat. What do I have to look forward to?

Recently, I scheduled a colonoscopy. I'm 53. I suppose it was time.

If you know what a colonoscopy is, you don't have to be reminded. If you don't, better to be spared the travelogue.

The concept is not attractive. What's the most uncomfortable thing you can imagine? That's a colonoscopy.

The prep involved buying a product called MoviPrep. The name is self-explanatory. You would have thought it was Silver Oak Cabernet Sauvignon and on allocation. Rite Aid on H Street downtown was out of it and so were the other four Rite Aids.

I called Longs. They had one box left.

"Please hold it for me," I pleaded. "I'll be right over."

The instructions called for a fast the day before the colonoscopy. "CLEAR LIQUID DIET" was written in caps on the MoviPrep box. There was no part of that instruction they wanted you to forget. Not the "CLEAR," the "LIQUID" nor the "DIET."

Bouillon was allowed, chicken or beef flavor was fine, but "NO NOODLES" was capitalized. Somebody must have had a really, bad experience with noodles, and there was no way anybody ever wanted to repeat that one again.

No eating the day before? What was I going to do with myself? How was I going to be happy?

Of course, no food meant no wine. Why don't they just take away air. Water.

Turns out, they did. The day of the colonoscopy, four hours before the procedure, water was off the table, too. One more day and I would have been sucking on washcloths.

The prep starts the night before by mixing Packet A and Packet B into a clear plastic container along with a liter of cold water and then downing it within an hour.

A couple of suggestions. After you have downed the solution, you might want to excuse yourself from the common living area. It's not as if you cannot participate in conversations but, at some point, you may get that faraway look on your face similar to a baby who is planning to wreck his diaper.

The morning of the procedure, I mixed a second Packet A with Packet B and drank it. If the truth doesn't set you free, MoviPrep will. I felt as if I had been through a car wash and they had done a really good job of vacuuming the carpets.

I tried making friends with everybody in the waiting room at the Truxtun Surgery Center. This included the nurses. It was a weak move and people generally ignored me. Friends and colonoscopies are mutually exclusive. You can have one or the other, but not both.

I survived. We live on the razor's edge of the present, to quote a wise man who hadn't. At this stage, we cheat death one colonoscopy at a time.

A SMOKING DEAL

I bought a car. It was "new" except the previous owner had smoked for 14 years.

The price was good. Too good. After I had signed the papers, the salesman said that the car had been owned by a large, friendly woman from Texas, who had exercised the freedom granted every car owner, which in this case included smoking.

"The car has been sitting with the windows closed and the sun on it for a month," said the salesman when I asked him about it. "Open the windows and you'll probably be fine."

He was a friendly man himself, and like the silver-haired owner of the lot, a Scientologist. I spotted 15 or 20 books by L. Ron Hubbard in the small, cheery office that brooked the car lot. Some of the books had spaceships on the cover.

"I've never bought a car from a Scientologist before," I said, glancing at the bookshelf. "My experience with this car will determine how I view Scientology from here on out."

It was a weak threat. Both the owner and the salesmen knew as well as I did, that once I walked out the door, I would have all the God-given rights that a new car owner would have which, in this case, would not include returning the car and receiving a refund.

If I was trying to unearth some information about the car, preferably potential future problems, I had a better chance of doing so by boarding the spaceship and talking to someone with two heads.

In other words, this was a car deal. What made it even more imperfect was that it was a used car deal. In used car deals it helps to have faith, even if it's a ride on the spaceship with L. Ron Hubbard.

The fact was, I had a smoky car. It was a good car, but it was a smoky car.

I don't know about you, but ever since Google came out, I feel more optimistic about what is and is not possible. Smoky car? Google "How to get the smoky smell out of a car?"

Before I did that, I visited Pep Boys and the AutoZone. If anybody knew, they would.

"I bought a car from a smoker," I said to the man behind the counter at AutoZone in an effort to troll for both sympathy and common ground.

I didn't have to wait long for a response.

"I'm a smoker myself," he huffed.

My apologies. I too am a man of the open range, but might you recommend something more in the Ralph Lauren line than the current offering from the Marlboro Man?

I bought a bottle of Febreeze, whose motto was, "It's that fresh." I sprayed the entire contents in the non-leather component of the car's interior, and now when I open the car, it sings out to me, "I am too fresh."

Thus to Google. The fix-all for everything wrong in modern life. All you have to do is ask. I did and this time I ended up on The Frugal Life website.

"Monica" suggested leaving a dish of citrus peels in the car.

"I had a 'vomit on a very hot summer day' smell in my car and it went away in a few days with the citrus peel. The trick is to leave it until it dries out," she wrote.

Robin recommended "using some coffee (not already perked) and put it inside a sock. Tie the end of the sock. Then, just put it in the car, maybe under the car seat and it will take the odor out."

The strength of Robin's suggestion is that if the coffee doesn't work, you can brew the coffee, sock and all, for quite a flavorful cup.

A third writer suggested placing "a bowl of white vinegar in the car and leave overnight and the next day the smell should be gone. This worked for a friend who had some meat fall out of her grocery bag in the trunk of her car in the summer in Florida and found it a few days later by following her nose."

Currently, the car has three bowls of white vinegar from Smart & Final in it. I trust this will have some effect. If not, a ride on the spaceship may be in order.

BLIND FAITH

For a dog that can see, it's athletic — but for a dog that can't, it's just this side of inspirational.

I'm talking about Poco, the blind chocolate lab puppy, and her willingness to jump in the back of the truck so we can drive to Beach Park where we take a walk.

When I say blind, I mean blind.

We've had her a year and she's crashed into about everything a dog could crash into and still live. Gates, chairs, tables, benches, trees, Gennie — the black lab that can see — pant legs and stairs.

Besides running into everything, the reason I know she's blind is that when I turn on the back porch light early in the morning, she doesn't blink. Night, day, she doesn't know one from the other.

Poco lives, as many dogs do, for her daily walk. Most dogs would trade their right paws for 15 minutes in an open field or a river bottom.

When the keys are jiggling and it's clear we're heading for the truck, she runs around like crazy in the backyard, banging into Gennie, suddenly forgetting the locations of the backyard furniture that she has memorized.

The walk starts with a two-minute drive to Beach Park. At the beginning, I put the dogs in the front seat of the truck— but dogs make their living being messy, dusty — and if they have their way, muddy.

I have a pickup, it has a bed and for an eight-block drive, the dogs can hang their heads over the sides and enjoy the wind.

Gennie has no problem jumping into the back of the truck. Poco could jump, but she couldn't see.

After a week or so of hearing Gennie jump into the back of the truck, Poco tried it herself but the angle was wrong. She crashed into the tail lights and fell back on the curb. I picked her up and put her in the truck.

The next day, Poco tried again. This time she knocked into the end of the tailgate, but dragged two paws up on top. Progress.

For the last six months, she has been jumping into the back of the truck.

Occasionally she misses. One time she sailed past and landed on the right rear tire. Mostly, she jumps, soars and makes it with 6 inches to spare.

Recently, one of the children e-mailed and another talked to me across the breakfast table. The gist of both conversations was that life was hard. Hard and not getting any easier.

It's not just the age. Or being in your 20s. I thought the same thing last week.

When this happens, I think about the blind dog. The blind dog jumping into the back of the truck that she will never see. She doesn't know that it's a '92 Chevy, beaten up, dented, inside door panel loose, and yet my pride and joy.

All she knows is that that truck is the ticket to whatever little freedom she has: the park, the river bottom, pools of sprinkler water on the dirt path, and things that smell.

She'll risk whatever unscarred flesh she has left on her face, and there isn't much, because she wants, but more importantly she believes.

She has faith. Even when she bangs her head and falls backward.

If a blind dog can do it, it's hard to believe that we can't, too.

I said this to the children who were having bad days. When those days are my days, I repeat it to myself. Blind faith. For some of us, if we didn't have blind faith, we wouldn't have faith at all.

NEIGHBORS FROM OUTER SPACE

Like most people, we have a wonderful collection of neighbors that includes the old and wise, families and then the children who infuse the neighborhood with warmth and purpose.

One of our more interesting neighbors recently moved in after leaving a club where he had been a guest for several years. He appears to have been well thought of, although a measure of the club's regard did not include allowing him to take the orange jumpsuit he was fond of wearing while he strode around the grounds.

This young man is friendly. He is quick to say hello. He is also vigilant about making sure his trash toters are curbside on Thursday, trash collection day.

He is popular. Friends stop by. Morning, noon, night and sometimes, even in the middle of the night.

Well wishers include the police, who often pay their respects twice a day. It's hard not to feel honored by their presence as they drive slowly by.

The lights are always on at my neighbor's house. Even at 3 a.m. It's festive. If Google Earth is looking for a house in Bakersfield on which to fix its coordinates, you could see this one from outer space.

We're duds. We're asleep by 10 p.m. in our house. Maybe 11 on the weekends, if things are really rocking. It takes New Year's Eve to see midnight.

Not him. Nor his friends. Every night is New Year's Eve for

them. It's nothing for them to be up until 2, 3, and 4 in the morning.

I'd love to have his energy. He is go-go-go. His friends are lively, too.

A guy like that can really make you feel like a slug. Most of us are a mess if we get less than eight hours. He never seems to sleep. I'd be surprised if he slept eight hours a month.

He gives every indication of being retired. Not that you can hold that against him. We ought to attend his seminar. Not yet 30 and done with the work world. He has it wired.

Speaking of wired: Prior to moving in, another young guy lived in the house. They remind me of each other. Maybe they are brothers.

The former tenant was energetic, too. He had the best looking lawn in the neighborhood. Sometimes, he'd mow it three times a week.

He'd mow it one day and then mow it the next day, too. His lawn looked like Pebble Beach. He made ours look like we were growing corn.

I don't know what his secret was, no matter how many times he mowed the lawn, he never got tired. He gave the impression that he had enough energy to mow the whole neighborhood and then take on the park, too.

I've wondered what happened to him. He lived there for a few months and then somebody moved in with him. One day he disappeared.

It's almost as if he got eaten or something, because then there were completely different people living there and then they got eaten, too. It was all we could do to keep up with the plates of zucchini bread.

A couple of days ago, the police paid our present neighbor a visit and took him on a drive. They liked two of his friends well enough to invite them, too. It must have been a long drive because they haven't been back since.

HITTING THE PAVEMENT

Saturday morning, I hurtled myself off my bike on Edison Highway going about 25 mph. I was running out of things to write about. Why not get hurt?

Actually, if I had realized how happy it would have made some of my friends, I might have considered taking a dive earlier.

I was riding in the back of a 12-man pack heading west on Edison between the packing sheds and Vineland. Somebody yelled. Yelling in a pack of bike riders usually means obstacle ahead.

In this case, it was a white truck that had swerved into our lane in order to miss a radiator. If you're looking for a radiator, there is a free one on Edison Highway.

Yelling was followed by braking. The rider at the front of the pack braked, followed by the rider behind him. It was basically a fire drill on skinny tires.

The news came to me late. It was like being the last peasant in the kingdom to hear that the king has been overthrown, the troops defeated and the bloodthirsty horde is marching toward your hut.

It would be romantic to think that there is a certain grace to a 52-year-old man sailing over the handlebars. It would romantic, but it would be inaccurate.

In free-fall, body parts compete with one another to make contact with the asphalt. In short order, I buried my left shoulder, right thumb and head.

My head (without a helmet, I would be playing first base on Gerald Ford's softball team) may have hit the pavement twice. During the trip to Memorial's ER, I asked Zac, a friend who was giving me a ride, three times whether he was helping with the triathlon.

He was either helping or he wasn't helping. My asking him

three times wasn't going to change that.

Sue met me at the hospital. She almost fainted when she saw the blood and the dislocated right thumb. I can't make her heart go pitter-patter with charm or good looks anymore, but I can stop her cold by bleeding.

When you get over the stupid part of it — no easy jump for people of good sense and sound judgment — there is something heroic about bleeding in front of one's spouse. That's why when people ask me what happened, I don't say, "I fell off my bike," I say, "I crashed."

"Fell" sounds like something a clumsy person does. "Crashed" is like something that happens when you are barreling through enemy lines. "Crashed" is Paul Revere. "Fell" is your grandmother in the shower breaking her hip.

I was lucky at the ER. Roger Almklov, an old Racquet Club friend, was on duty. His hair has turned white, which really gives him an air of "he knows what he is doing."

Richard, a friend, came by. He had a cast on his hand too, so he was looking for company.

"Don't you want to put a full cast on his arm?" Richard asked the doctor. "Why don't you put one on his leg too?"

I didn't think he could get any happier, but I was wrong. Before they stitched up my right thumb, the nurse irrigated (a farm-friendly word for bled) the wound. I thought Richard was going to break into an operatic aria.

Being hurt was good for business. I had eight voice mails when I got home. People were moderately concerned with the health of the rider, but more concerned about the well-being of the bike.

I have painkillers that I'm afraid to take. "Afraid" because I know they'll work and I'll like them. The next thing you know, I'll be walking on North Chester trying to get a refill.

For the refill, one hand will do just fine.

Anything slip-on becomes your friend. So do all things buttonless. You seek left-handers with whom you may shake hands.

SUE GETS RICH

I'm rich. No, not me, my wife. She's inherited $150 million.
At least that's what I thought a week ago. I had a dream.
This was more a pipe dream than I have a dream dream.

Talking about your dreams is risky. Who cares? Even people
who care don't care. Dream recitation stampedes people toward the
exits quicker than a plume of smoke and a fire alarm.

Most dreams are too complicated to talk about. At the time,
they make sense and seem more compelling than a Martin Scorsese
movie. However, in the retelling, they make about as much sense as
the first 700 pages of Ulysses.

This one was simple: Sue inherited $150 million. If the dream
lacked clarity, it may have been because it was unclear whether the
money came from a rich uncle whom she had not known, or a rich
uncle whose wealth had surprised her.

You see what I mean. Who cares?

I went back to sleep. I made a note to tell her when the no-sleep
zone was safely behind us. I looked forward to starting the day
with good news, news that would distract her from the steady leak
we have in our dining room ceiling.

I told her. She was happy. She said that after she crossed off a
couple of destinations on her travel list, she was planning to give a
million dollars to Operation Smile, the charity that repairs childhood
facial deformities, and then a million to Doctors Without Borders,
the foundation that does pretty much what its title suggests.

"I might give something to the children, but they would have to
earn it over time," she said.

We were making progress here, because what is better than
eliminating cleft palates and then curing what was left? Secondly,

who doesn't want to give a passing nod to the next generation?

That left out one person. Me. The person to whom she was married. If I hadn't eaten four chocolate brownies with dried cherries the night before, there wouldn't have been a dream, $150 million dollars and bequests, either philanthropic or personal.

I realized that the money put me, and her too, in an awkward position. Should she give me a lump sum figure or should we discuss an allowance?

The allowance thing bothered me. There was something slightly demeaning about it. I have pride. Not a lot, but some.

No one gives an allowance without expecting something in return. What would I be expected to do that I was not already doing?

Be nice all the time? I can't do that. That's impossible.

I could shoot for every other week. Or maybe, once a month. But every day? I have a better chance of becoming district attorney.

Giving me a lump sum could be a problem for her. No one likes to give away a bunch of money. Not to your spouse. They might get ideas, ideas which may or not include them.

We were stuck. She was loaded and I was trying to figure out how to shovel some off the pile. Once again, money both solves problems and creates them.

Solve that problem and you could be rich.

WHAT'S NEXT

The returns are in. The votes are counted. We just don't know who won yet.

I'm talking about college applications along with the acceptances and rejections.

It's quiet in our house. Unless the wind rustles the wind chimes, you don't hear much. The mood is one of a decision yet to be made.

This is a tricky dance. Parents know that if they have a preference, the surest way of seeing it honored is by keeping quiet. Even indirectly. The misdirection play may work in football, but in college, suggestions, no matter how subtle, can backfire, leaving parents a sputtering mess.

Choosing a college looms over everything else in the house. It is like the light in a solar eclipse. Everything looks funny.

First, the choice of schools involves geography. North or south, east or west. Not that there is a finality about where you start—my older brother transferred three times. He changed schools like some people change socks.

Parents want to weigh in, but can't. What if their children go far away, meet somebody, get married and then choose to live in the Georgia lowlands? Where we have to board two planes, take the ferry and then walk the last four miles.

The faraway thing is one consideration. The other reason for the church-like quiet in the house is that any decision—close or far—may be an acknowledgement that things are changing. Several months from now, life will be different.

High school friends will stay home and leave home. There will be a bunch of goodbyes followed by a bunch of how-do-you-dos.

There will be hot breakfasts, but they will probably be served in clean new cafeterias. The bacon-and-egg sandwich will not be waiting in the oven. Your parents will be eating that sandwich. That one and the one after that one.

Your bed? There might be an exercise machine in its place. A meditation mat. A wet bar set off by some snappy neon.

When you return to the house, you may not recognize the place because we've turned it into a nightclub. We might have a water slide and a miniature golf course.

Yes, things are going to be different. There is a natural arc to life and after 18 years, it is time or almost time to leave and chase rainbows. There is uncertainty but joy, too, in the freedom.

However, for now, this is all we know. This is all they know. Though home may be getting ragged around the edges — translation, my parents are not as funny or interesting as they think they are — they are a known quantity and can be counted on for not being that funny or interesting. Bank on it.

The privilege of deciding which college to attend signals closure for this stage of life. Given that parents are not likely to get funnier or more interesting in the next couple of years, it's not a bad time to move on.

Wait though. You might be surprised. When we put up the neon and stock the wet bar, things could get interesting around here again.

GRADUATION AND THE GIVING TREE

Tuesday, I read "The Giving Tree" to a kindergarten class at Olive Knolls Christian School. Everything you need to know about life is in that book. It's age appropriate no matter what age you are.

I looked at those restless 6-year-old faces and sensed they were not only straining at the reins to start summer vacation but eager for the next step and the next step after that.

They might as well have been flying up several flights of stairs without stopping or touching the ground.

This past January, I handed out schedules in the BHS cafeteria as I've done every semester for the past 10 years or so. I had the B's. All of a sudden, I looked at the empty seat to my right and Thomas, our youngest, was sitting there.

"What grade are you in?" I asked.

He looked at me. He smiled. Senior, he said.

Senior? Impossible. That staircase wound nearly to the sky.

Parents don't know a lot, but we know one thing. No matter how steep the climb or how fast it goes, we love our children completely and blindly. This love seems ancient, as if from the beginning of time. If not the beginning of time, at least the beginning of our time with them that, for some of us, goes all the way back to Memorial Hospital.

Parents know another thing. Someday our children are going to break our hearts. Whether they've been good or bad. Good or bad has nothing to do with moving on.

Thursday was graduation. What makes graduation tender for parents is that we are saying goodbye too. Not just to our kids, but to their friends, their teachers and the other parents with whom we've shared this time.

We say we'll return to the school, but you wouldn't bet the house on it. I suspect high school will be like most of the schools they've attended. Once gone, the school becomes a curious relic from another lifetime.

We say we're going to keep in touch with the other parents, we want to, we mean to, but there is the post-high school continental drift. The plates shift. They go to Antarctica and we go to the Caspian Sea. High school, junior year, elementary school, kindergarten. Done. Come September it will be somebody else's turn to fill the seats at the talent show, watch the History Day performances or pass out schedules in the school cafeteria.

Four, six or eight years from now, I wish them the same luck we've had. That they might be sitting in that cafeteria trying to find a student's schedule, turn and have their beautiful son smiling at them.

Yes, it's all there in "The Giving Tree."

We've given our leaves, apples, branches and trunks to the lives with which we've been entrusted.

Given the opportunity, we'd do the same thing all over again. Maybe next time it wouldn't go so fast.

DUDE

Be careful when you enter a room. Tread cautiously. Especially if teenage boys are present and in conversation.

You might enter as a mother, a father or a sister and leave as a dude.

This summer, my nephew, Chris, is living with us. He has a painting business. This makes his father, who lives in the Bay Area, happy because his son can now experience a Bakersfield summer rather than something that has the fragrance of the ocean in it.

Chris and Thomas, our youngest, are usually articulate. They also are generally delighted in each other's company as are many cousins.

So delighted that when they come together after the day's conclusion of summer jobs, there is a high-spiritedness that manifests itself into a quick round of "dude," or in some cases, "Hey, dude."

The word "dude" is not surprising as a form of address. The late Norm Hoffman, the fitness guru and BC professor, would, as a matter of course and affection, call friends "dude," but there was a difference.

Hoffman would use "dude" in the greeting, in other words, the first part of the conversation; then, if it was necessary, revert to the name of the person to whom he was speaking.

This is not the case with Christopher and Thomas, nor with any of their friends who pair off in what turns into a high-energy exchange.

"High energy," because after the initial pair of "dudes," the conversation picks up steam and in less than a minute, one dude has become two, four and then, it's a dude frenzy.

The dudes come as relentlessly as machine-gun fire. The cousins are like a pair of gunfighters, both guns unholstered and blazing, firing away at each other as if dudes were bullets and there was an infinite supply.

The air is painted with a rainbow of dudes — high, low and in between. By the end of the conversation, the cousins have been thoroughly duded up.

It's almost competitive and given the skill and alacrity with which the dudes are delivered, is not far from an exhibition sport in the Olympics.

Observers are advised to remain clear of the exchange at the risk of, either purposefully or accidentally, being duded up themselves.

No one can keep up the frenetic pace, and after a minute or two, the hail of dudes slows down and then ceases.

The conversation may stop but something has happened. Important information has been exchanged, some of it having to do with being dude-worthy.

There is a brotherhood of dudes and you are either in or you are not, and if you are not there is no formal application process.

Best to be an observer. Best, however, to stand clear, so that one does not risk being caught in the crossfire.

Really. Dude.

DOMINIC

Bring it.

He did until he could bring it no more. Then it was up to the people who loved him, and they were legion.

"Today, the road all runners come,

"Shoulder-high we bring you home."

Dominic Ambriz died August 16 after a 31-month fight with glioblastoma multiforme brain cancer, an aggressive disease.

He grew up in our downtown neighborhood and went on to become one of the rising young toy designers at Mattel. His parents — Don and Jane — could have given lessons in how to raise kids. Other parents admired their cool — especially during the teenage years when many of us were either freaking out or popping corks — and most of Dominic's and his sister Amy's friends would have put themselves up for adoption had they known they would end up in the Ambriz family.

I heard the news at LAX via text. That's how news comes these days.

Dominic's fight was over. The incredible struggle that had

amazed his friends and confounded the doctors who had predicted a steeper decline and an earlier passing had come to an end. Patients diagnosed with GBM, as it's known, struggle to live 18 months. Dominic lived almost twice that long.

He was surrounded by friends. Scoob, his loyal girlfriend, had signed on after he had been diagnosed.

His parents, Don and Jane. All parents love their children, but some are put to the test. During the final lap, they slept by his bedside in a cot for 60 of his last 62 days.

To say Dominic Ambriz was a fighter is like saying Lake Tahoe is blue. It's blue, but it's even bluer than you think.

After he was diagnosed with cancer, Dominic did the following things:

Completed the Mud Run in Bakersfield, finished a half marathon in La Jolla and two triathlons in San Luis Obispo, a full marathon in Albuquerque, lifted more weights than the Chinese woman who won the Olympics and went back to work as a toy designer for Mattel, his beloved company, whose president fought for his medical care and paid for it at the end.

Dominic also wrote and illustrated a second book for his niece, which followed the first one, "Madison the Fearless."

No one with a brain tumor looked better and accomplished more. Dominic forced his healthy friends to re-evaluate their programs and mothball their excuses.

If anybody is worried about this 20-something generation, they shouldn't be. His friends rallied and did so in the way that his generation does. Led by his longtime friend Marshall Coyle, they set up a Web site that delivered the updates, rallied the troops and stoked the love and collective will of everybody in his circle.

Given Dominic's strength and fortitude, the tag line for the site was "Bring It!"

"I had asked him if he was up for the treatments that he had just described to me," Coyle said. "He said, 'Yeah, as long as I have my boys, bring it.'"

We knew Dominic's parents when they lived in Bakersfield and owned Earthworm Studios.

Don was a gifted calligrapher and graphic artist when people were still drawing by hand. Jane framed pictures. Dominic created our annual haunted house in the neighborhood (always including the younger kids in the construction), made masks for Halloween and eventually helped create the Pixel Girl and the Plush Toys for Mattel. His sister, gentle, beautiful Amy loved children and made working with them seem like art.

More than anything, the Ambriz family was close. Not much could pry them apart.

"While in college, Dom was sitting in a child psych class — the topic was effects of childhood," said his father, Don.

"They went around the room and fellow student after student talked about what an unhappy childhood they all had. Dom was really taken aback. He said, 'Are you kidding me? I had a great childhood!'"

BHS led to the Otis Art Institute which led to five satisfying years at Mattel. Dominic made an impression there, not only with work, but with little kindnesses that make work bearable.

"The most inspirational thing Dom did for me was that he drew this little football player and it read "who R U callin small", after I had my son who was only 1lb 8oz," wrote fellow designer Tina Atkins.

"I kept that drawing hung in my son's isolation room the entire four months that he was in the hospital. That drawing (which probably took him five minutes to draw since we all know how talented he is) provided me such joy and inspiration during a very difficult time in my life."

Saturday, a celebration of Dom's life was planned for the cafeteria at Franklin School.

Dominic was a student there, and his father designed the marquee in front of the school using his son's tow head as inspiration. Like Dominic, it probably took Don about five minutes to illustrate it.

For Saturday's celebration, the marquee read: "Dominic Ambriz Bring It!"

Dominic was 28. He never gave up. Never stopped bringing it.

Now it's up to the rest of us.

TAKING THOMAS TO COLLEGE

We were fine until we drove by the Claremont Hotel and turned on KFOG five minutes before we were to move him into his dorm room.

"Landslide" by Fleetwood Mac was playing.

"Well, I've been afraid of changing
Cause I've built my life around you
But time makes you bolder
Children get older
I'm getting older too
Oh, take my love, take it down ..."

I had to put on my dark glasses. His mother and I were like Tang—we dissolved. He probably thought we were nuts already and "Landslide" swept us off the edge.

Last weekend, we took Thomas, our youngest, to college. I learned a couple of things, the first being that boys are different from girls.

With Katie, the oldest, we fogged the windows all the way to Fresno after we dropped her off at Davis. With Thomas, you can blame it on Stevie Nicks, but that's about as far as it went.

More parent education. You spend your whole life learning how to say goodbye. What a thing to get good at.

Bittersweet is the word. Sweet because that's what he's been. Bitter because sweet has moved on.

He asked what would be for dinner at breakfast and ate everything on his plate, even if it was green. He was company on the denim couch for his father during Lakers, Dodgers and middle-of-the night World Cup games.

I learned something else. He was lucky. His father was fine, but he had this mother. Hard to imagine anybody loving him more, but that could happen someday.

The night before, we stayed with my brother in the East Bay. At

10:30 p.m., Thomas opened the sliding glass door into our room. He started talking about how much he was going to miss not having cats around. The conversation was about cats and it wasn't. He could have slid the door closed, but he didn't. Everybody says goodbye in their own way and in their own time.

Before we left Bakersfield, he sat with the dogs on the back porch for a few minutes. He stroked Gennie, the black lab, and talked softly to the blind dog.

It was 103 degrees when we loaded the truck in Bakersfield. Sixty-two when we unloaded it in Berkeley. This boy was smart in more ways than one.

"Dad, I don't know if I'm going to come back for summers," he said.

I couldn't argue. I'd sweated through my shirt and Jockey shorts. Just expect a roommate come next July.

Besides the three skateboards, Thomas had less stuff than his older sister. It took an hour to set up his sixth-story room. It took me almost as long to figure out the U-lock on his bike.

T-shirts folded and put away, we went to lunch at Crossroads, an airy cafeteria where Thomas will be eating most of his meals. Lunch, which consisted of turkey, roast beef or ham sandwiches, a tomato bisque soup, Lay's Potato Chips and chocolate chip cookies, was free. That's probably the last free thing we'll get from Berkeley.

It was time to say goodbye. His mother hugged him twice, the second time because the first was shorter than she would have liked. I went for one, but found myself not in a big hurry to let go.

Two hours later, his mother texted him. The parent guide said to give your freshman some space, and his mother deduced that two hours was space enough.

"I just had an awesome bike ride," he wrote back.

Before going to bed, I sent him a text message that read: "Sweet dreams, son."

His response was "Thanks Dad. You too."

Parent guide be damned.

THANKSGIVING FLOW

Thanksgiving was interesting. "Interesting" can mean thought-provoking, prickly or may indicate adventure found, but not necessarily sought. Our Thanksgiving included all three.

The house could not have been cozier. The candles were lit, the fire had been burning for hours, two bottles of champagne had been drained and the children were home (save one, who was involved in a minor family skirmish).

The turkey had been carved, the gravy thickened (the secret lies in the giblets) and the spread was laid gaily on the counter in all its Thanksgiving glory. The last of the guests had filled their plates and were headed into the dining room when someone said, "Oh, Dad."

A noise followed, not necessarily a Thanksgiving noise like that of a cork leaving a bottle, but a water noise like that from a small river that had been dammed, but was dammed ("damned" works, too) no more.

"Well, I'll be," Herbie noted. "Hot water is coming through the light fixture in the pantry."

I put down my plate on the beautiful Thanksgiving tablecloth and walked over to the pantry. Herbie was right. Hot water was pouring through the fluorescent light fixture. We were grateful for hot water, especially when we had a full house, but normally we preferred it cascading through a shower head or a faucet, rather than a light can.

I generally like myself, but every so often just a sliver of self-doubt enters my mind and I wonder, "Is it me, or does everybody have cars that glide silently to a stop on country roads miles from civilization and hot water rushing playfully through a light fixture that heretofore could have been described as recessed?"

Had I been paying attention, I might have noticed that this Thanksgiving was destined to have been "interesting" from the start.

Thursday, at 1 a.m., 17 hours earlier, Thomas walked into our room and said, "Dad, can I talk to you?"

Yes, you can, but 1 a.m. indicates that the subject might not include the Lakers and the wonderful beginning to their season.

"Nothing bad happened to me," he said as I followed him to his room. "But. ..."

"But" is like "interesting." When those two roads come together, even GPS can't save you or provide a map. You could be tumbling off on an adventure or end up the main character in an epic Russian novel.

A 4-foot section of Thomas' ceiling had collapsed. Large chunks of plaster covered his bed, bedside table and his chair (he was not in the bed at the time).

The incidents—the hot water and Thomas' ceiling—appear to have been unrelated. The common denominator was me, and that thread cannot be underestimated unless this thread runs through everyone's life.

I don't recall eating much at Thanksgiving. However, I do remember looking around the table at one point at John, my father-in-law, whose face seemed to say, "I'm glad I'm going home in an hour."

After turning off the water to the house and using two or three dozen towels to mop up the water that ran like a warm and inviting river on the carpet, we ate an absolutely wonderful meal. Men who knew how to do things came later, and within three hours, the pipe had been fixed and we now enjoyed hot water in the usual places as well as a clear view of the ceiling right down to the 108-year-old studs.

Life is interesting. No buts about it.

IS THE TREE STRAIGHT?

My favorite part of the holidays is centering the tree in the tree stand. Normally, I'm the down man; in other words, I'm under the tree with my hands gripping the trunk of the tree, while I'm polishing my face on the hardwood floor.

"Is it straight?" I yell in a tone of voice that indicates the tree's rectitude is a matter of national security.

"No, not yet," says a voice faint and far away.

The voice faint and far away is the voice of the decider. Until the tree is straight, the down person, who is both splayed out and doing neck lifts in order to see over the green plastic Christmas tree stand will remain the down person.

"How about this?" says the down person, inhaling a line of fresh Douglas fir needles up his nostrils.

"No, now it's leaning to the left," says the voice less faint and more exasperated. "Can't you pull it to the right?"

I could if I wasn't blind, lying on my hip, and scissor-kicking as if I were being hanged sideways. If I were standing up, a position I've gotten pretty good at, I could jerk the tree left, right, center or flip it upside down and jam it into the Christmas tree stand Heavenly Angel first.

"Ok, it's straight," the voice said. "Can you hold it right there?"

I'm not sure. Not only does holding it right there entail not breathing, but it also means turning the screws in the stand until they are firm against the trunk.

Some of the screws go in nice and easy, but others require machine-like strength. Tightening the more stubborn screws is akin to snugging up the lug nuts on a flat tire with your teeth.

It can be done, but subsequent medical attention might be

required.

At this point, the cat decides to pay a visit to the down person. Isn't this fascinating, she thinks, and meows to confirm her interest.

Normally a quiet moment with Callie, all soft and furry, is welcome, but when your neck veins are throbbing and you are in the process of stripping most of the skin from your hands in an effort to tighten the screws and keep the tree straight as a lamp post, there is little attention left to devote to a cat that does not have a full schedule to begin with.

We bought the tree from the Bakersfield College baseball team and picked it up on a practice field on a cold, overcast day. This is our 10th year and the players never seem to age, a reason to go to school but never graduate.

I can't tell one tree from the next, but it seems unsporting to pick the first one so we had our helper, a catcher on the team, unfurl another tree, and then we bought the first one anyway.

This is the first year we have decorated the tree without the children. As they got older, they became less viable in the Christmas tree decorating arena. We tried to borrow a couple of little girls down the street, but they were busy decorating their own tree.

The children are coming home for the holidays. That makes us happy. I'll be the down man for that any time.

Wii WIN

I can no longer say I've never played a video game because now I have. Recently, a neighbor invited me to his house because one of his daughters had received the game Wii as a birthday present. For some of us, fools maybe and bad sports certainly, it's almost a badge of honor to say we've never played a video game.

"I've never played a video game," I've said many times, searching for something that would distinguish me from the teeming masses although the teeming masses who play video games seem to be pretty happy doing so.

Playing it seemed a painless way to deal with my video game virginity as well as honoring the advice older people give younger people about staying young: Learn something new every day. I hadn't learned anything new that day or the day before so Wii would have to do.

I can't tell you much about the game except that it involves your TV screen, a console that you plug into the TV and a remote with which to hit a baseball, golf ball, tennis ball or whatever game the player chooses.

"You can get a really good workout playing this game," said 10-year-old Maggie.

A workout? I thought video games were supposed to be a rather sweatless enterprise. Something you did in a dark, air-conditioned room until all hours of the night. If I wanted to sweat, I could go outside and sit in my car.

I chose tennis because I've played tennis and when you're playing a video game for the first time, you want to limit your losses. I didn't want to be embarrassed by a 10-year-old girl, or worse, her father.

Without going into numbing detail, you take the remote, and start swinging at a ball that appears on the screen. I don't know how any of this works and I'm not even really curious. I just didn't want to make a fool out of myself.

Lord, you can get a sweat going, especially when you have a serve and a set of ground strokes as powerful as mine. However, even with my obviously exceptional game, I managed to lose the first set to a sixth-grader.

OK, I'll swing harder in this next game. I bent my knees and I lunged toward the screen. Crack. I had backhanded the TV screen with the remote.

I pushed the start button to activate the next point. Nothing happened. I pushed again. Still nothing. I handed it to Maggie because she is a kid and she understands these things but she couldn't get the remote to work either.

The room became quiet with the sound of dashed expectations. It appeared that I had broken the remote and ruined a child's birthday present. If I had had a rope and a lick of self-respect, I would have hung myself from the oak tree outside their family room.

I looked online to see if there were other problem players like myself. This is what I found.

"We have received some reports that when consumers swing the Wii Remote with the original version of the wrist-strap using excessive force and accidentally let go, the cord connecting the controller to the wrist strap can break, potentially causing the Wii Remote to strike bystanders or objects."

There was nothing about breaking a little girl's heart.

I wrote the friend a check for $40. That may or may not cover it. I've learned something about playing video games. You sweat, and they're not cheap.

THOMAS THE VEGETARIAN

"I predict Thomas is going to last about a week as a vegetarian," said Sam, Thomas' ye-of-little-faith brother.

The scene was the recent holidays when our four children made a pilgrimage home. Family dynamics are interesting to begin with but never more so than when someone has made a lifestyle change.

Thirty-five years ago, my sister went to college and returned a vegetarian. She loved horses and one day she may have made the connection between horse and meat, even though, in our house, the twain never met.

Pam stayed strong even when her brothers said things like, "Mom's pot roast sure tastes good. I'm not sure I've ever had better pot roast. Especially with the carrots and onions swimming like happy children in the meat gravy."

Thomas had not really become a vegetarian, he'd only given up eating red meat.

Red meat has a PR problem, starting with the word red. Red is fine until you put it in front of meat and then you might as well just say "red meat served with a side of blood."

Blood is fine, but people would rather have it live in the blood bank than sneaking around the outskirts of something they're considering eating. Without the specter of blood, I think more vegetarians would eat pot roast.

When the children are home, I look forward to cooking a "Big Country Breakfast." At its best, the Big Country includes scrambled eggs with cheese and Italian spices, homemade muffins studded with raisins, cranberries and dried cherries, coffee and of course the centerpiece, the thick-sliced Applewood Smoked Bacon from Trader Joe's.

For the non-meat eater, pork is a swing item.

It passes the "it's not red" test by being pink. Pink is a nice color. I have a pink shirt, and my friend Russ has a closetful.

"That bacon sure smells good," Thomas said.

Yes it does, son. I don't know if you noticed but I cooked two packages of bacon for the Big Country Breakfast.

Should you decide to include bacon in your diet, your share will be between six and eight pieces, or about one-fourth of what the Friendly Cafe in Oildale used to include on their plates that were larger than truck tires.

"Red meat has not been hard to give up," Thomas said. "But you know what I really miss?"

What?

"I'd really like a Double-Double from In-N-Out," he said. "I've been thinking about a hamburger."

A good hamburger will make you forget all about pot roast.

Vegetarians are sacrificed daily on the altar of two pure beef patties decorated with lettuce, cheese, a slice of red onion and presented on a sesame seed bun.

"What is pepperoni?" Thomas asked later, minutes before he was to meet friends at Pizzaville, for what appeared to be shaping up as a pepperoni pizza.

What is pepperoni? I'll tell you what pepperoni is.

It's good, especially when it's sizzling hot on top of a bed of melted mozzarella with a real thin crust platform.

Thomas went to Pizzaville. He was gone awhile. When he returned, he was smiling.

I didn't ask. That's between him and the colors of the rainbow.

TRONCONES AND SHARKS

Blood had been flowing lately in Mexico. That wasn't good. However, I couldn't see any reason to add to it.

"Dad, I think I saw some sharks," Paul said.

It didn't matter who Paul was. What mattered was that last week I was sitting eight feet away from Paul on a surfboard at a break called A-frames near Troncones, Mexico, about an hour from Zihuatanejo.

Paul is my cousin Bea's 19-year-old son, and "Dad," is his father, Ron. Along with Thomas, our youngest, we were a foursome in the water.

Now, I like — perhaps even love — Ron, Paul and Thomas, but when someone yells "Sharks!" a tight-knit group suddenly becomes four guys rooting that the other three get sideaches.

Whereas the mention of a singular shark will make you sit straight up on your surfboard, sharks — the plural version — causes surfers to levitate clean off their boards. That's not a flock of frigate birds, those are four surfers who have heard the word "sharks" and have sprouted wings.

Maybe Paul was crying wolf, and maybe he wasn't. Last April, there were three shark attacks in the Troncones area — two fatalities and one in which a surfer lost a digit. Which digit, I'm not sure.

These attacks took place about 30 miles and five small Mexican villages south of where we were, but this is not like Shafter and Bakersfield separated by 7th Standard Road and a sump.

For a tasty treat, sharks will swim to Shafter. If they're still hungry, watch out, Kingsburg.

Why was I wearing those stupid black rubber booties? I had put them on because I was worried about stepping on a sea urchin should I have ended up inside on the rocks. However, a guy sitting on a surfboard with his legs dangling innocently in the water with booties on his feet looks like something in the two-legged blubber family.

"Let's stay together while we paddle to the boat," said Ron, Paul's father. "The sharks are more likely to attack a lone straggler."

"Stay together?" I'd forgotten I was with anybody. Forgotten that I had a cousin, a family, children—one of whom was a few feet away.

Thomas was 18. A hundred years ago, 18-year-olds had told off their fathers, married their cousins and fought two wars. If they could kill a deer with a flaming arrow, certainly Thomas could paddle to the boat with a shark chasing him.

Thomas, it's time to grow up. Soon, you'll be on your own. "Soon?" Now that the shark was on our tail, consider "soon" to be now.

As we paddled to the boat, there was a mighty war being waged inside my heart. On the one hand, this was my flesh and blood that

I was surrounded by.

On the other hand, flesh and blood was what the shark was chasing and certainly if I were a shark, I wouldn't want some tired, 54-year-old with a history of depression and distressingly low iron levels.

Ron had never been sick a day in his life, and the boys were young. Go ahead. You choose.

"I think I still see them," Paul said.

You do? Where? We were 15 feet from the boat. You don't think a shark would get us when our hopes were high and we were so close to the boat, do you?

Who was I asking? God? Mr. Wizard?

Our surfboards clanked against the boat. For the record, we did let the teenagers pile into the boat first. We're adults, right? Our families are Job 1.

For the record, those sharks were porpoises. Sharks, as I learned, prefer to travel alone.

Alone. That sounded familiar.

INAUGURATION

WASHINGTON — Tuesday was like the snow day. Remember 10 years ago? Everybody in Bakersfield was up early and happy.

This time I was in Washington. Barack Obama was sworn in as the 44th president of the United States. There wasn't any snow, but it was cold and everybody was happy — even my mean Republican friends from Bakersfield who called me asking what it was like to be there.

I'll tell you what it was like. It was a good day to be an American. Any kind of an American.

I learned some things from this inauguration. First of all, never borrow another man's boots. My friend, Harry, loaned me his because they were warm and sturdy.

They were also size 12's. I'm normally a 10, but when it comes to buying a pair of boots I might use once, I can fit in anything from a woman's size 6 to a size 22.

My advice would be to stick with your own shoes unless you're looking for a case of kneeitis.

The trip was my wife's idea. Sue's a sucker for any trip. She keeps her suitcase on the cedar chest at the foot of our bed because it reminds her where she's been.

This wasn't a hard sell. Watch the History Channel in person. What made history possible was that her brother lives in Arlington, 10 minutes outside of D.C. Free boots, free place to stay and our own Congressman Kevin McCarthy made it a trifecta by setting aside free tickets. Kevin doesn't have much use for me, but he likes Sue and sometimes you have to ride your spouse's coattails.

Tuesday morning started at 6:30 with a walk toward the Potomac — Arlington Cemetery on our right and the Iwo Jima Memorial on our left. We went across the Memorial Bridge, around the Lincoln Memorial and up the Mall toward the Capitol.

As if on cue, a reporter from National Public Radio stepped out after we crossed Memorial Bridge and asked me what I was feeling. I rose to the balls of my feet ready to lay down some inspirational commentary, but I started with four straight clichés and then summed it up with a couple of indecipherable sentence fragments. Good thing I wasn't getting sworn in.

"You look like you're very emotional right now," the reporter said, microphone extended. "I think you have tears in your eyes."

"Actually, I'm so cold my eyes are watering," I said, as the mike fell to her waist.

The path leading up to the inauguration ceremony was chaos. Now I understand what people say about Washington being gridlocked. Streets were closed, routes were barricaded and there were many mosh-pit sorts of moments that had everything but somebody getting tossed in the air.

On any other day, there would have been fisticuffs and cross words. Not Tuesday. Tuesday was snow day, Washington style.

Our seats were in the yellow area. They must like McCarthy back there. Not only did we have chairs, but we were about 200 yards from the Capitol steps.

The purple section was right behind us, separated by a barricade. The barricade was good because they had to stand. You never know about those standers. They may be watching the inauguration, but what they're really doing is thinking about how good your seat would feel.

I sat next to an older man from Oklahoma. I asked him if Obama had won Oklahoma, and he told me no. I told him he ought to work a little harder next time.

I'm not much for pictures, but when the Capitol is in front of you and the entire government on the steps, I can't pass that one up.

Aretha Franklin sang, Rick Warren prayed and Obama spoke.

I lost it when Warren was talking about the son of a former slave. Hard to believe a black man could become president. Even when Obama had his hand on the Bible, it was hard to believe it was going to happen.

Obama said what he always says and I believed him, like I always do. Afterward, some of my loyal Republican friends called, and I sensed for a day, maybe they believed, too.

The sun came out before the ceremony started. It was almost warm. After the last prayer was uttered, the clouds covered the sun, the wind picked up and people buttoned their long coats again to keep out the frigid air.

It was a great day. And it didn't even snow.

WAKE UP DAD

My dad came to visit. He's good company. It's a treat to have him. We played tennis, walked and ate some dinner. He does all three well.

We gave him his own bedroom. I mean, the man is 84. He can't be sleeping on the couch.

Like most men of his generation and work ethic, he used to rise at the crack of dawn. There wasn't much choice. You either started in on the day or the day started in on you.

That's changed. Early has gotten later. It was my understanding, and prior visits have indicated as much, that he now rises between 7 and 8, although I couldn't put my finger on what his average is.

This became pertinent because on Day 2, 7:30 a.m. came and went and so did 8. Then, it was closing in on 8:30.

I'd never had these thoughts before, but I've never had an 84-year-old father either. What if, I thought? What if last night's dinner — barbecued chicken, sourdough bread and salad — was Dad's last supper?

Mortality is one thing, but this was tricky. I have three brothers, two sisters and a mother, and if Dad was in there not moving as much as he used to, what would I tell them? "He was fine when he went to bed, he even had a piece of dark chocolate after wiping out a bowl of Cherry Garcia. His appetite was excellent."

However, no matter what you say to your siblings, you're playing defense. They are thinking, "We never had a problem when he stayed with us."

Instantly, you're the son who rowed their father to the other side of the lake. Hallmark doesn't make a card for that. It's a hard one to live down when Dad doesn't show up at their house for

Thanksgiving dinner.

Ten minutes later, I put my ear to the door. It was now 8:40. He hadn't slept that late since returning from World War II.

I couldn't hear anything but the fan. At least that was still working. He always liked his circulation.

I wanted to open the door, but I didn't want to wake him up, just in case he was wake-upable. If he wasn't, I wasn't in a big hurry to go in. I needed time, and some good excuses to compose "My Speech to the Family."

No matter what you say, they're thinking it's the chicken. You didn't cook it, he ate a bad piece, contracted chickenitis and then went to bed with his beloved fan and that was all she wrote.

It was now 8:45. Please Dad, wake up. Even if you don't feel like it. Even if you can't.

People have done that before. Gone into the white tunnel, seen grandma, then woken up and enjoyed a steaming bowl of Cream of Wheat.

I had to open his door. It was almost 9. At 9, I might as well just call Ray Mish.

I opened the door. He was lying under the covers. That was good, but not definitive. Lots of people lie under the covers. Some of them even get up.

Was he breathing? I looked for the telltale signs of the chest heaving and the shoulders rising up and down. If there was air being exchanged, I didn't want to walk in the room, and go to his bedside, because he might knock me out. He was a Marine, and I never even played one in dress-up.

I think I saw something move, but my eyes weren't that good. I could have been willing those shoulders up and down. Please, Dad, give me a sign. A cough. Kick your leg out. I know you still remember your lines from Damn Yankees.

I closed the door. Fifteen minutes later, I heard some stirring. I saved him a blueberry bagel. That and the rest of the chocolate bar.

A HOME FOR TENNIS

When Howard Welty wore out his right arm and announced that he was going to learn to play tennis left-handed, I thought, sure. Like that's going to happen.

Not only was he past 50, but in the tennis world (Rafael Nadal being the exception here), you're either right- or left-handed. Right-handers secretly fear left-handers because the serve moves in confounding ways, and left-handers distrust righties because they feel outnumbered. It's like being a redhead in China.

Welty, who died last week at the age of 91, not only switched hands but became a competent lefty. He joined the dark side and never looked back.

I learned two things. First, don't bet against Howard Welty. The second, don't underestimate the power of yes.

Seeing his picture in the obits last week reminded me once again what a wonderful place the Bakersfield Racquet Club was growing up. The club, as far from fancy as you could get, was built in 1948.

Tennis is endearing because every match has a storyline. However, what made the Racquet Club important to those of us fortunate enough to pass through its gates was the opportunity to learn from players older than we were. And, you could always find someone older.

Consider Fred Hagist, one of the best players of his day. Matches with Fred, when he was on his game with his dead-level flat ground strokes, could take 30 minutes, and that included the warm-up and the Bob Lynn (grape juice, 7 Up, orange juice over crushed ice) afterward.

One day, when I was in the midst of a teenage funk (shortly after he beat me 6-1, 6-0), he said, "When I'm feeling bad, I find that shopping makes me feel better."

I've heard that since, mostly from women, but at the time, it was a revelation coming from a man.

From Gentleman Jack Lynch, there were other lessons. Jack always beat his younger opponents 6-4, 6-4, no matter how good or bad they were (he wanted you to go home feeling optimistic about your prospects). Jack demonstrated that exquisite sportsmanship was possible, at least in somebody else.

Jack had a firm handshake and blue, blue eyes that did not waver.

Andy Davidson, one of the teaching pros, taught frugality. Andy always brought his lunch to work, and when Steve Williford took over from him, it was one of the first pieces of advice Andy gave him.

Lake Lovelace, the founder of the club, was a terrific storyteller. Lake was as kind as he was determined, determined that Bakersfield should have a home for tennis.

From the nooners, we learned how to kid. Needling is an art and was as important to a nooner's success as a spin serve or a cut forehand.

What's valuable about a racquet club, and really any setting where people of all ages come together in play or work, is that knowledge, humor, manners and tradition are passed between one generation and the next.

To do so, sometimes that means you have to play left-handed.

SHORT STACK IS NOT SHORT

Order the short stack. One pancake, not two. Two's been tried. Ordering two pancakes at the Red Wagon Cafe is like trying to get served at a bar around closing time after you've consumed 30 White Russians. You should be done, even if you aren't. And you might have to call in a Cub Scout troop for help.

Things are shrinking. Retirement funds, icebergs and height — if you're into your seventh decade. Not the short stack, and with a name like short stack, you'd think that would be the first thing to go.

Bob Smith, a friend, had told me about the Red Wagon in Shafter. Bob's not a big guy, but he can eat like a big guy, especially after he's ridden his bike 75 miles (which he does quite frequently).

I was looking for two things: breakfast and a story. If the story didn't work out, I figured breakfast would.

Last Friday, we drove to Shafter. Bob's a regular and the Red Wagon is like Alaska: It helps to have a guide.

It's easy to miss. The Red Wagon is an old railroad car on the corner of Beech and Burbank, red paint peeling. From the outside, you wonder if it's big enough to have tables.

Like any local restaurant or watering hole, there's a seating chart. Don't try to change it. Learn it and fit in.

"The regulars sit on the south end and the new people on the north side," said John Ray, a retired pipeline welder. "Let me put it another way. The sinners go right and the Christians left."

Bob and I went right. We weren't regulars and had no business going right, but we didn't know any better. We either didn't know any better or we didn't know ourselves as well as we thought we did.

For a moment, it appeared that in order to be a regular, you had to have one eye. Ray recently had cornea surgery —his second, and he only had one good eye. Andy Sharp, who was not only a regular but a world-renowned expert on every subject, was a one-eyed pilot. The people in the Red Wagon were friendly, but they don't see as well as they might.

Bob Wiebe, a Shafter farmer, told me to ask for Sharp, if he was, and Andy is always in. I just had to wait my turn.

"Andy is an authority on small matters," said Ray, the pipeline welder.

The Red Wagon has it covered in at least two ways. It's hard to leave hungry. However if you do, and you raise a fuss and get arrested and need to get bailed out, look on your coffee cup. It reads "Absolute Bail Bonds 877-7-We bail."

Strong women make a place like the Red Wagon. Usually, it's a mother-daughter team. Here it's Shirley Epps, and her daughter, Jamie Colbert. Carolyn LaRue, Shirley's sister, owns the place and drops in occasionally. Sondee is the cook, and she makes a mean strawberry cake, but let her bring it up first.

Thelma & Louise, or at least a part of it, was filmed across the street at Collins Market. The Red Wagon is the kind of place where Thelma and Louise would have eaten and felt comfortable. Given how they were feeling, they could have sat anywhere they wanted. North or south.

It doesn't pay to be in a hurry at the Red Wagon. The short stack with three pieces of bacon (mine) and the bowl of oatmeal (Bob's) took time. Slow food gives customers time to catch up.

Friday's news: Andy Sharp held court on the pistachio recall. Bob noticed that the ceiling fan was spinning backward and that was discussed too. Ray, the retired pipeline welder, talked about his tomatoes.

"I have about 100 tomato plants (Ace, Celebrity, Early Girl, Fresh Salsa, Porterhouse)," Ray said. "In the summer, I sell them to the restaurant. Sometimes, I eat for free."

More news: The Red Wagon, an old 500 Series train car, was

dragged to its present location in the '40s by Wasco's Hoyett Smothers. Hoyett was a character. You have to be a regular to know why.

Lastly: The Red Wagon opens at 4 a.m.

Those customers are serious. They're also farmers, oil field workers and people who may not want to talk about what they do, especially at 4 a.m.

Finally, Epps brought the food. You had to be kidding me. Where was the plate hiding? That pancake looked like it was resting on air.

"A truck driver stopped in once and ordered a short stack," Sharp said. "When it came, he looked at it and said, 'That will get me to New York.'"

Mine was one hungry pancake. It lapped up syrup like a thirsty dog laps water after a long run. I kept pouring and the pancake kept drinking.

After I'd finished, they brought a piece of jalapeno corn bread. It was sweet, dense and a loyal part of the bean, potato and cornbread Friday lunch special.

An hour and half later, no one had moved. The regulars have done the moving thing before, and it may not have worked out that well. They liked it where they were just fine.

MEETING HUNTER'S PARENTS

"I want to talk to you about something and I don't want you to get mad," Sue said.

You don't want me to get mad? I'm mad already because you're about to say something that is going to make me mad, and then you're going to claim diplomatic immunity because you warned me first.

"I want to talk to you about what you're going to wear when we have lunch with Hunter's parents," she said.

Hunter is Katie's current boyfriend. Katie is our daughter.

With previous boyfriends, we had never been invited to meet the parents.

"What were you thinking of wearing?" Sue said.

It depends on who you are asking. If the question is directed at Cooperative Herb, then it could be a pair of light gray wool slacks, a long-sleeved blue-checked dress shirt and a pair of black penny loafers.

If you are asking Independent Herb, it could be brown yoga pants, a blue Wavelengths T-shirt and a pair of Sanuks.

Why was Independent Herb sticking out his prickly head? Hunter's parents had kindly invited us to lunch and I.H. was going in with a monumental chip on his shoulder. Independent Herb was acting like 2-year-old Herb without the winsome charm of a toddler.

"I was thinking about wearing the gray pants and the blue shirt," said Cooperative Herb.

She paused and then, mustering great patience, said, "You're not going to wear that blue gingham shirt, are you?"

Gingham? What do you mean by gingham? You're not talking

to a farmer on his way to a barn dance. I bought this shirt in a shirt shop. A fancy men's clothing store. This shirt was folded, pinned, had cardboard wrapped inside the collar and was enclosed in a clear plastic bag.

"Maybe you could wear your black T-shirt from the Gap," she said.

Cooperative Herb likes the black T-shirt from the Gap. C.H. looks good in that shirt. C.H. thinks he could model for the Gap.

"Would you mind getting your black shoes professionally shined?" she said.

You just can't stand prosperity, can you? C.H. likes the black Gap T-shirt, but Independent Herb is not fond of paying someone to shine his shoes. I.H. can shine shoes. By the time he's done, you'll be able to see the reflection of the Milky Way in them.

"Please, it would mean a lot to me," she said.

Cooperative Herb dropped his shoes off at the car wash to be shined. Then he went to Charlie's place to get a haircut. Sue hadn't even asked about the haircut. That was a gift from Cooperative Herb. C.H. is like that. C.H. is lighting the peace pipe while Independent Herb is beating the war drums.

"How much for the shoes?" I asked the shoe shine man when I returned to pick them up an hour later.

"Eight dollars," he said.

Eight dollars? That was half of what my haircut cost. Cooperative Herb wanted his shoes shined, not turned into ostrich boots. For $8, I.H. wants a shoe shine, a foot rub and an oil change.

Hair cut, shoes shined, clothes pressed and attitude adjusted. We were ready. Ready for what the weekend would bring.

HE FOUND HIS WAY

Graduate?

A few years ago, I wasn't worried about him graduating. It was living that had us crossing our fingers so hard they cracked.

He was a wild child. Sometimes you get one. When it happens, all you can do is hold on for dear life.

The wild ones are drawn to the edge no matter what kind of counsel parents, grandparents or teachers give. We might as well try to undo gravity as to knock them from their orbits. Parents can cajole, convince and advise all they want but their words are scattered in the winds of adolescent rage.

I remembered my brother Derek, Sam's uncle, saying, "He's going to be something if he doesn't end up in prison."

We were in that fraternity of parents who don't know how it's going to end, good, bad, or worse. We heard it, repeated it and tried to believe it.

I almost lost it last week when I saw the invitation lying on the counter. Blue, stylish and crisp.

"Please join us for a graduation celebration honoring Sam Benham."

We didn't have a party when he graduated high school. We were happy that he moved out of town, but there were no party streamers. Mostly, we exhaled for the first time, in what seemed like six years.

This time, our family will celebrate at his godmother's house in San Diego the night before he graduates. Proud? Yes. Mostly we are grateful.

There is nothing automatic about parenting. No guarantees. You're simply trying to get them through. Deliver them alive to their 21st birthdays or to whenever they stop bouncing off walls.

Bad things can happen to good kids who are going through rough patches. Kids who make a mistake and never have the chance to make their parents as proud as they might have.

This boy was easy to love until he was about 10. Sound familiar? Ten might be 12, or 13, or whatever. You get the idea.

After that, we still loved him, but we were doing it on fumes. We loved him but liking him was almost more than we could manage.

As a parent, that's when you find faith. Or darkness. Or both.

In this case, it's faith that a miserable present will turn into an acceptable future.

It was the story of the Prodigal Son except Sam did some of his "riotous living" at home. Sam eventually came to his senses when he was on his own. Life had to teach, and it did.

Sam's moment came three years ago when he crashed into a telephone pole in San Diego, totaled his car and lived. That was his turning point. Survival meant delivery. Delivery meant knowledge, knowledge meant change and change power, to quote P90X's Tony Horton.

Sam changed jobs, changed paths and changed attitudes. The jagged edges smoothed. He became all business and, this time, business was good business.

We are lucky. We have good kids. All of them. It's hard to favor one over the other.

Sam's Sam. He is the first to call his mother on her birthday. He is the one who sends her a Valentine's card. He doesn't like a dirty car and he bristles when people mess with his stuff.

Graduation. It took six years. Six going on 24.

He walks in his commencement ceremony on May 22. We'll be there. So will his whole family, including two sets of grandparents who never lost faith.

Five days later, I turn 56. I've already gotten more than I asked for. My heart is full. I've graduated, too.

POT IN HONDARRIBIA

Vacation was Paris, Normandy, Brittany and Hondarribia, Spain, which is inside the Spanish border on the Atlantic side.

Hondarribia is Basque first and Spanish second. In five days, we didn't see one Spanish flag. They spoke Spanish, but their hearts appeared to be elsewhere.

Basques? We know the Basques. Weren't we from the land of Wool Growers, the Noriega Hotel, sheepherders and the Basque picnic?

I made Bakersfield my calling card. In conversations with waiters, shop keepers and strollers, I kept repeating, "I live in Bakersfield. We have lots of Basques there."

That fell flat. Not only had they not heard of Bakersfield, but I had the sense they thought any Basque who had left Hondarribia, San Sebastian or any other part of the gorgeous Basque country shadowed by the Pyrenees, studded with forests and spilling into the ocean, was not in full possession of his senses.

The Basques were easy to pick out because they are a dark, rugged people who, as I discovered with my calling card comments, do not suffer fools lightly. They look like they could survive in an ice storm, extreme fog or in a frigid ocean with a blustery gale in their faces. If you engage them in a long enough conversation, by the end of it, a clean-shaven man will have grown a full beard.

The Basque language would be easier to understand if it didn't have so many X's and K's. An occasional X or a K is fine, but too many in the same word or sentence causes the uninitiated to roll over on his back and put his feet into the air.

I stuck with 20-year-old school room Spanish. After a few days and six meals, I was clearly fluent. In a cab ride home after dinner from San Sebastian to Hondarribia, where my cousin Bea had eaten a leg of lamb big enough to drive a railroad spike, I saw what appeared to be a marijuana dispensary.

I asked the cab driver if marijuana was legal. I couldn't think of the work for legal so I took a shot on "legal" but I might have said illegal. When that didn't get a response, I rained the rest of my vocabulary on our cab driver.

The cab went quiet and Thomas, our youngest, who can actually speak some Spanish, shushed me and whispered. "Dad, he thinks you're trying to buy some pot."

Thomas quickly changed the subject to World Cup soccer.

Thankfully, there is no language barrier when it comes to food. Basque cuisine was incredible—inventive, fresh, beautiful presentation, great use of seafood — and nothing like the Basque food we have here, which has its place in the comfort food universe.

There were only two off moments with the Basque food. The first was the sweaty cheese that the Parador (state-owned hotel) served as part of the breakfast buffet. I don't like sweaty cheese because a sweaty cheese is a cheese that is working too hard. I want my cheese to be cool and relaxed.

The second disappointment was the lamb I ordered in a restaurant in Hondarribia. It was delicious, but it wasn't any bigger than a chicken leg. That leg was to a leg of lamb what a Shetland pony is to the Budweiser horse.

Between the tiny leg of lamb and dessert, I visited the bathroom. European plumbing can have its own personality and sometimes includes a Where's Waldo moment when it comes to locating the handle. Normally, the handle is on the top of the tank, sometimes on the wall behind it, but on the tiny leg of lamb night in Hondarribia, I couldn't find it anywhere.

After a few minutes, I raised my hands to the sky and beseeched God to tell me where the handle was. As I looked up to the heavens, like a sinner in one of El Greco's paintings, I saw a string hanging from the ceiling.

I pulled it. Although the ceiling didn't open and the angels didn't spirit me to my heavenly home, the toilet flushed.

One day, we drove across the border to Biarritz, France, and rented surfboards. There were four of us — Thomas, cousin Ron, his son, Paul, and me. New beaches are frightening because who knows what kind of sea monsters they have in Europe at the bottom of the ocean with open mouths and sharp European monster teeth?

Finally, Thomas paddled into a wave. Then Ron. Then Paul. My turn. Either I had to take off on a wave or hoist the white flag.

I waited for a wave that didn't look like it could hurt me too badly and then I paddled in. I stood up faster than a European surf champion and promptly jammed my left foot in the deck pad, broke my middle toe and then somersaulted off the front of the board.

I bore my fate stoically. My Basque friends do not complain.

NORMANDY

I picked up the rock. It was round, smooth, and there are a million like it on every beach in the world.

These rocks were green and jewel-like when wet, and gray and dull when dry. Without thinking, I slipped it in my right front pocket. My friend, Jim, a student of history and red, white and blue from tip-to-top, might like it.

"I'm surprised there are any rocks left," Ted said. "As many of them as people pick up."

He was right. I looked at Sue. She had a rock in each hand.

Most people don't pick up smooth gray rocks. Unless you're on Omaha Beach looking out to sea. That rock felt like a different kind of rock.

"After the war, my father said he would never swim in the Normandy beaches again because he knew what it took to take those beaches," Ted said.

Ted was Ted Malindine. He was our guide recently for a D-Day tour that included Omaha Beach, Pointe du Hoc and Sainte-Mère-Église (the famous town where paratrooper John Steele's parachute caught on the spire of the town church) and the American and German cemeteries.

It's humbling. No matter how much time has passed. No matter how much smart aleck you have in your soul.

What you do is pick up rocks in the rain and wonder where the tears come from.

If we were made of money, and schools sat on oil wells and diamond mines, history would be taught differently. Especially World War II history. Consider the history of D-Day, June 6, 1944, when the Allies stormed a nearly 50-mile stretch of beach, landing close to 156,000 troops and where eventually more than 425,000 Allied and German troops were killed, wounded or went missing.

This history lesson could be quiet. Rows of white crosses and Stars of David in the cemetery, which run endlessly in straight lines in every direction. Crosses and stars dressed up with American flags ready for the D-Day ceremonies a few days later. Quiet except the fluttering of thousands of flags in the Normandy breeze.

Reading is one thing and it's a good thing. Libraries are filled with excellent books about World War II. However, if you are fortunate enough to see the plane in person, the words become pictures. And those pictures have sons in them.

It's easy to forget because the war was fought so long ago by our fathers or grandfathers. They are older now. They have been older as long as we have known them.

They weren't then. They were boys. Each cross —American, German, Australian, French, and English — was a son his mother would not make Sunday breakfast for again.

Ted, our English guide, framed the tour that way.

"You two boys are about the right age," Ted said, to our son, Thomas, and his cousin, Paul, 20 and 21 respectively. "Although most would have been younger. They were scared, they were seasick and most had never been in battle."

That got their attention. Their mothers' too. Their fathers just tried to keep their sunglasses on and pretend like they were looking for snipers still ensconced in church towers.

It makes you think about the difference between generations. These guys stormed the beaches of Normandy. We may not be quite as sturdy.

After the tour, Ted took us to his hundreds-year-old Norman farmhouse, which he shared with his wife, Linda. His father, Edward, had been one of the British War Office photographers in France, Britain and northwest Europe from 1940 to 1945. Ted showed us photos of Stalin, Churchill and Truman, as they decided how to administer punishment to the defeated Nazi Germany, which had surrendered nine weeks earlier.

His father had photographed Hitler's bunker and there was one image of Ted's father draped in Hitler's medals. After we looked at Edward's photographs, Linda brought out six silver forks and a silver bowl with AH engraved on the back.

"When we were first married, we used these all the time," Ted said.

Mementos from the war. Some have part of Hitler's silver service. Others have smooth, gray rocks that turn silvery blue when washed by the tide.

P90X

A while back Rudy, a friend of mine, started P90X. If you've watched late-night TV or the informercials on Saturday morning, you've probably seen the ads for P90X or fitness programs like it. They usually come with three equal payments of $39.95, a bonus book and several jaw-dropping before-and-after pictures of people who have completed the program.

Realize this: the people in the videos are not like you or me. They are fitness aliens from Planet Perfect. Although they have work visas that allow them to live here, we are unable to visit their planet because they eat people like us upon arrival.

Rudy looked good, not like a fitness alien, but healthy. Fifty-six was on my horizon. It wasn't too late to have one of those beach boy bodies, was it?

I have a philosophy. I try not to spend more than $50 for any piece of fitness equipment, other than a bike, which can land in the small jet range. Like everything else, you can find somebody who bought what you want, and didn't use it.

Craig's List. I found a computer technician at Vanderbilt University in Nashville who had one new in the box. Sixty bucks, $10 more than I like to spend, but $70 less than it cost new.

P90X came in a handsome black booklike package, 12 DVDs strong. Ninety days of muscle confusion.

Muscle confusion. That sounded sexy. It was like jazz, replete with syncopation and unexpected riffs.

Every day featured a different DVD. Each session lasted for about an hour. Tony Horton was the leader.

"I wish he wouldn't dye his hair," said my neighbor, Sally.

What makes you think he dyes his hair? Can't a 50-year-old

man have black hair? His muscles may be confused but his hair knows exactly where it's going.

"I don't like the way it stays in place and never moves," she said.

What is it about women and wind-blown hair? They prefer men who look like they've put their head outside a car window at 90 mph. What's wrong with slapping on some Vitalis?

Tony is pure cornball. When you're working hard he says, "That's where the money is."

When he thinks you may be drifting into heart attack range he'll say, "If you need a break, take a break. I take one, you can too."

Tony is flanked by three or four fitness aliens, both men and women, and after going through the DVDs a couple times, you begin to wonder who is romantically involved in the group.

Tony, who is the leader and who has all the great lines as well as stiff hair that doesn't move, is popular. I wonder about some of the other people. Do they want to be Tony? Are they conspiring to knock him off his yoga mat? Roll out their own line of sleeveless, tight T-shirts?

The Yoga X DVD was an hour and a half. Want to feel your age plus 20? Dip into a yoga routine.

I couldn't even do some of the pre-positions before you do the position. Sit on the ground and cross your legs. No, I can't do that.

Wow, what happened? How did I get so stiff? The only one I could do was plank because it's a warm-up for rigor mortis.

I'd always made fun of yoga classes in rest homes. Thank goodness I'm not that feeble, I'd thought.

I am that feeble. The only thing I lack is flexibility and balance, the two main tenants of yoga. I was an ideal candidate for chair yoga and perhaps by my next birthday, I might crash my way to the floor.

The only thing harder than the yoga were the pull-ups in the back and shoulders DVD. I did three pull-ups and then almost ripped the bar out of the doorway and tore the house down trying for the fourth. I did about eight push-ups. The fitness aliens did 40 and their hair didn't even move.

Apart from being weak, inflexible and ready to topple over at any moment and pile drive my head into the carpet, I'm doing great. Fifty-six is coming soon. Beach boys beware.

HAT'S OFF

Big Al has 27 hats at home and has owned as many as 50 at once. He'll do everything with hats, except wear one at work, even on Big Al Avenue.

Work is the Emporium Western Store (founded in 1909), and Big Al Avenue is his corner of the 19th Street shop, where Big Al stretches, blocks, steams, fits, trims, shapes and cuts fedoras, Stetsons and good old-fashioned straw hats.

Big Al — last name Gonzales, but no one uses it — has been the hat man for the store for 46 years. His clientele stretched to England, Germany, Spain and Australia (a group of McFarland farmers and cattle ranchers moved to Australia in the '60s, hence the connection).

If you are a hat wearer, there may be no bigger honor than to have your hat size scribbled on a piece of paper that rests in the wooden drawer on his work bench, where Big Al keeps sponges, a steamer, Super Glue, presses, levelers, dyes, a small anvil and a clean towel on which to rest the hats.

Tony Curtis' hat size is in there. So is Buck's, Merle's, Jack Palance's, Chuck Connors', the great rodeo rider Ty Murray's, and a host of others.

Say you aren't famous. Even if you are, you are a new customer looking for just the right hat. By the time you weave your way from the entrance of the store past the tables with straw hats for $29.99 and $39.99, through the racks of shirts with silver buttons, the Justin boots, and, finally, onto Big Al Avenue, the man you're looking for will have you sized up within an eighth of an inch.

"Most men are a size 7-1/8 and women, a 6-3/5," Big Al said.

Tony Curtis came into the store years ago when he was filming a movie in the area with Erik Estrada. Curtis bought a Stetson Gambler (The Royal Flush) and a pair of deerskin roping gloves that he used for driving.

Curtis liked the gloves so much that he called back and ordered two more pairs.

"Call me Tony," Curtis said, figuring anybody who could call his head size from 20 feet away ought to be someone with whom the star was on a first-name basis.

Big Al (his brother is former Assemblyman Ray Gonzales) credits two things in the last century with stoking a global interest in hats. We can thank Teddy Roosevelt for Panama hats (they are made in Ecuador, at night, when it is cool). He donned the classic hat— worn at a jaunty angle, of course — after the Spanish-American War at the end of the 19th century.

"The Urban Cowboy sold billions of hats for us too," he said of the 1980 John Travolta movie.

Big Al said Buck Owens visited the store the day before he died to have three of his Rand's custom hats creased.

"He was standing around waiting and he saw a photo on the wall I had of him and Brad Paisley," said Big Al. "He said, 'Big Al, let me sign that picture for you.' He was in good spirits."

The most expensive hat he's ever sold — and he's sold three of them, two to the president of Ramona's Mexican Food Products — was the Stetson Diamante, 1000X for $3,999. The hat is made from chinchilla, ermine, mink and beaver, has diamonds in the hatband and comes with a Plexiglas display case. Big Al guessed the food honcho's hat size before his two bodyguards could adjust their sunglasses.

Hat fitting is as much an art form as it a science. Big Al steers customers away from hats that don't fit their faces or whose size and lift may overpower the rest of their bodies. Thus the phrase, "All hat and no cowboy."

When I tried on a couple of hats, Big Al moved me from the Stetsons into the Panamas. I was no Ty Murray, and he knew it.

The hat business has changed in recent years. In the 1970s, there were more than 20 stores in Bakersfield selling Western wear.

Now there are less than five. Big Al's hat clientele includes farm workers, labor contractors and former rodeo princesses who have become grandmothers. Big Al (his own family includes three boys and three girls) is almost reverential about his clientele, although having a sense of humor helps too.

"People ask if the hats have a lifetime guarantee," he said. "I say yes. If something goes wrong with the hat, we'll kill you."

Big Al's stature is such that he has a hat named after him in the Milano Larry Mahan line called the "Big Al." Even better, Bill Lee's Bamboo Chopsticks, where he eats four times a week, has a dish named after him called the "Big Al Special" that features sweet and sour pork with an egg on top.

Big Al is 76. He is the hat man. The only one on Big Al Avenue.

THIS ONE DOESN'T CRY

On Friday, May 13, I was picking up some soft chocolate chip cookies from Jake's when Sam called.

"How are you doing?" I said. No sooner were the words out of my mouth than they'd been rendered inappropriate, given the silence that met them.

"Terrible," he said. "Jeff died last night. He ran into the back of a truck on I-5 and was killed instantly."

Jeff Jordan was buried last Wednesday at Greenlawn Southwest under a sky that couldn't make up its mind between rain and sunshine.

They were best friends in high school, and when Sam left our house his senior year over differences that I can no longer recall, he stayed at Jeff's house with Jeff and his mother, Janelle.

They were brothers in a way that brothers sometimes can't be. Jeff was wonderfully mechanical, could fix motorcycles, dirt bikes, work on cars and seemed destined for a profession that required both uncanny sleuthing and raw mechanical reasoning.

Life wasn't smooth, but no matter how rough it got, Sam and Jeff stayed in touch.

Both were fiercely loyal and fiercely loyal to each other. Sam was like a second son to Janelle, visiting her faithfully when he returned to Bakersfield.

"I'll be coming home," Sam said.

That night, Sam's sister, Katie, baked him his favorite cookies, Rocky Mountain chocolate chip, and put them on his doorstep in Pacific Beach.

When she didn't hear back, she got worried. Turns out, she'd left them at the identical house next door. The boys inside had had a few beers and ate them before reading the card.

When they read the card, they bought a dozen fresh-baked cookies and took them next door with the card and introduced themselves. That's one way to meet your new neighbors.

Two days later, Sam came home to Bakersfield. Juan did, too. Juan, Jeff and Sam were a team. No one rooted harder for Jeff when he was down than Sam and Juan.

Jeff had been doing better — a girlfriend, a job at a refinery, and a renewal of his faith.

Sam arrived home that night at 1:20 am. I know, because I looked at the clock, and his mother held him until 1:21.

For the funeral, Sam wore black pants, a blue shirt, a white tie, and black shoes. He had typed up something, which he had put in his pocket.

Rain. The funeral director had extra umbrellas and passed them out to those who hadn't taken refuge under the blue canopy reserved for family and close friends.

Sam refused the umbrella. His blue shirt and black pants began to get wet. Rain streamed down his face and it was hard to tell where the rain stopped and the tears began.

I'm not much one for coffins, but Jeff's was beautiful. Dark mahogany, silver handles. Flowers on top, and later, a friend placed his black motorcycle helmet to be buried with Jeff.

It was a Catholic service, and after 20 minutes, Jeff was committed to eternity.

Juan and Sam walked together to the microphone. Each spoke beautifully but differently. Juan has a poet's soul, and Sam is more practical.

"Jeff was the first friend I ever had who told me he loved me," Sam said.

Later, he said, "Jeff always looked good when he left the house, fresh, and so I wanted to dress up today. Jeff, I hope we're representing you well."

After the service, Sam hugged Janelle and Jeff Sr. No one wanted to let go.

Everybody has their way of getting through these things. Mine is childish but it is what I hold onto: Take forward the best of the person who stays behind.

That night, after the funeral, Sam and Juan were back at our house. Good soldiers, friends and guardian angels who would have given anything to have guarded Jeff in his final hours.

I can't remember what was said, but Sam, who was sitting in the brown leather recliner, leaned back and smiled.

I knew that smile. Jeff. He had a great smile, and he saved it for the people he loved best.

I SAY YES

Two weeks ago, I was called in to work on a Sunday. The phone rang. It was an 858 area code with a number I didn't recognize.

The last time I had received an unfamiliar call from 858, it was the ICU nurse at Sharp Memorial Hospital telling me Sam had been in an auto accident.

"Mr. Benham, this is Hunter," he said.

Hunter. Katie's boyfriend. Although I was tempted to ask if I could call him later when deadlines had relaxed, there was something in his voice that made me keep the phone pressed to my ear.

He sounded emotional. Nervous. Embarrassed, too.

"Would you mind if I spent the rest of my life with your daughter?" Hunter asked.

There are moments of clarity in life. Moments that stop time and sweep everything else away. When they come, they deliver a burst of emotion that scrubs the decks.

"Katie is so sweet," he said. "Would it be OK if I married your daughter?"

Would it be OK if you married my daughter? No, it wouldn't be OK. It would be wonderful.

"I know I should have driven to Bakersfield and done this in person," he said.

If I were my friend Hank, you probably would have, but I am not, and a phone call will do fine.

"Hunter, I would be delighted if you married my daughter," I said. "You've stood by her and seen her through some rough times."

I stopped there. I was on a roll, but if I kept rolling, I'd roll right off the cliff.

"Mr. Benham, there is one thing," he said. "You can't tell anybody."

I can't tell anybody?

"I haven't asked her yet," Hunter said. "You're the first one I've told. I haven't even told my own family."

For once, I have some good dinner conversation and I can't say anything?

Friday night, five days later, the phone rang. I had put Hunter's call deep in the storeroom, to be retrieved at a later date like a jar of pomegranate jelly for future dining pleasure. I almost didn't answer it because calls on the house phone tend to be from Wells Fargo about a new product that I might not be ready to enjoy.

"Dad, Hunter asked me to marry him tonight," Katie said. "He took me to the beach at sunset."

I didn't act surprised. I couldn't fake that. However, I didn't have to fake the joy.

"Could I talk to mom?" she said.

There weren't many things that could pull Katie's mother away from Grey's Anatomy, however, this was one.

"Sue, your daughter wants to speak to you," I said.

I've seen her happier, but you'd have to return to the day Katie was born to get close.

News like this puts a spring in everyone's step. Grandparents, friends, cousins, even Katie's brothers, who like most brothers, are wait-and-see kind of guys.

A couple of days ago, the house phone rang again. It was Fred and Susan, Hunter's parents, and I had them in stereo.

I like these people. He's from El Centro and he's tough, self-made and intensely interested in history. Susan is good through and through and keeps Fred tethered to the earth.

They've been married a long time. Fred and Susan have raised three well-mannered boys and, with Katie, they will have a daughter to love.

Katie is engaged. This is fun. I say yes. We all do.

DEL MAR

Being on vacation is checking the real estate to plot the big move, fantasy-fueled as it might be.

This time there was a dandy little trailer in Leucadia, a quarter mile from the beach, in the Valley of the Dreams, 123 Jasper St., No. 17, for $132,000. I asked Ed Johnson, the real estate agent, if the owner would take back any paper.

"Yes," he said. "If you put down $70,000, he'll take back paper."

Seventy-thousand down? Ed, that paper sounds like green paper. I was thinking about $500 down and a 325-year mortgage. I kept the sales flier, but already I've torn out a quarter of a page to make a grocery list.

We've been going to Del Mar for more than 40 years. It seems funny to say that. Forty years is a long time, but if you have to age yourself, the beach is a good place to do it. Good because, although people age, the wind, sand and waves do not.

There is a moment when you know you've surrendered to vacation and mine happened while standing in the Bank of America in Solana Beach. The tall bald man at the front of the line with a Bluetooth in his ear began talking to the blond woman between us.

"Have you heard?" he said. "BofA is laying off 3,500 people and soon they will be eliminating another 10,000 jobs. They never should have bought Countrywide. Everybody knew it was a toxic asset."

The blond woman nodded and mentioned that HP was going through similar carnage. The woman and the bald man were playing Top This Disaster.

Bad news for both companies and their employees, but after several days of coastal fog, the sun had come out and it was 70 and glorious. Although Gadhafi was on the run and unemployment would soon crest 30 percent, I was in flip flops and a dumb hat and my memory had been wiped as clean as a new hard drive. I knew I cared about the world, but that seemed a long time ago.

While on vacation, we saw all the kids, hardly kids now that they are solidly in their 20s. In their teens, sometimes we had to drag them to the beach, but no more. Katie and Sam live in La Jolla and San Diego, and Herbie and Thomas flew in for a few days from the Bay Area.

We took the Christmas picture against the sea wall and they didn't complain when I had to change from a blue to a black shirt. Christmas pictures have been the occasion for mutinies in the past, but they know their mother well enough now and are old enough to recognize that since she has cooked 32,000 meals for them and given them a stunning childhood, they will give her the Christmas picture without comment.

They get along better. At one point, Thomas grabbed Sam, his sometimes-gruff older brother, hugged him and said, "Give me some love, Sam." Even Sam smiled.

It helps to have space; good vacation spots have that in common. A beach to spill out onto or a meadow and mountains in which to disappear; activities like walking, swimming or surfing that make people tired and help smooth the jagged edges.

We didn't have sun most of the time, but we didn't notice. The locals were concerned about it, but when you're from Bakersfield, sun is not a career goal. Cool is, and with the fog came plenty of sweatshirt-wearing evenings.

Putting on a sweatshirt for dinner. Jeans too. That qualifies as luxury.

I made my annual vacation Scrabble sacrifice. Sue beat me 10 of 11 games. The one game I won, she turned her letters in once, surrendering a turn, I had a bingo, I had the Z, Q and J and still I barely squeaked through.

New discoveries. We brought down a CD by Adele, the British singer. It's not a good idea to write off today's music. If you're inclined to do so and feeling grumpy besides, listen to Adele or "The Cave" by Mumford & Sons.

More education -- and on vacation often that can center on food. I brought a 3.3-pound carton of milk chocolate raisins. That's a lot of chocolate raisins, even if you like chocolate raisins.

I bought some amazing cinnamon bread and orange bread made by Greenlee's Bakery in San Jose. It was vacation bread, thick, filling with tons of icing. I brought a loaf home. This bread will make your toaster feel young again.

It was hard to say goodbye, mostly to the kids. They are fun to be with. It's harder to even remember when they weren't.

There is a trailer in Leucadia. The owner will take back paper. Green will afford you blue.

KATIE'S WEDDING

Katie was married last Saturday. It was thrilling. Her mother and I agreed that it was one of the happiest days of our lives. A friend told me he had run out of tissue before he walked down the aisle with his daughter, so before driving to La Jolla for the wedding, I went to H. Walker's and bought a six pack of handkerchiefs. I imagined myself heroically coming to my wife's aid should she lose it in the church.

Sue, the mother of the bride, received another French manicure the morning of our departure. Oh no, the French manicure had reared its head again. I would be carrying all the luggage. We didn't want to chip those nails.

We arrived at the Grand Colonial Hotel in La Jolla on Thursday afternoon. The valet took the car and I reached in my pocket for a couple of dollars. Tipping the valets each time they park the car can exhaust even the most patient father of the bride.

"Just give them one tip at the end," Sue said.

The woman is a genius. No wonder she was in charge of planning the wedding.

Friday morning, Sue and I went to the bridal shop with Katie in downtown San Diego. When Katie walked into the showroom after putting on her dress and her grandmother's veil, that's when I needed a handkerchief. Moments will sneak up on you, and that one did.

Later that day, we went to the La Jolla Country Club for some last-minute details.

My primary concern was the wine temperature at the reception. We had a meeting with the manager, Chendo. I started in on how cold I like the champagne and chardonnay, and prefer cellar temperature for the red. I'm sure this small, elegant man in a gray suit thought I was a lunatic.

Two nights later, Chendo came up to me with a cold glass of chardonnay.

"Cold enough?" he said with a smile.

Yes.

Late Friday afternoon, we had the rehearsal at Mary, Star of the Sea Catholic Church. Do I walk on Katie's left or right side? Right. I enjoyed the rehearsal. When you have a horse in the race, everything becomes fascinating. I will not be able to see weddings in the same way after viewing one from the inside out.

The best part of a celebration can happen in between the big events. The conversations you have in the car on the way down, breakfast with aunts, uncles and cousins from out of town, walking to Vons with Al (the best man at my wedding) on Saturday morning to pick up the 11 boutonnieres made with pink roses.

Start your celebration before the wedding.

I took two showers Saturday morning. You are allowed an extra shower the day of your daughter's wedding. I spent an unusual amount of time in front of the mirror because I didn't want to walk down the aisle with soap on my ear.

I wore a black tuxedo. It felt great. Why have I been fighting the tux thing all these years?

People look at you differently when you are wearing a tux. Men give you wide berth and women smile. Women know.

Saturday, at 1:25 p.m., I walked to Katie's room, No. 305, and knocked on the door. We were scheduled to take the limo to the church, four blocks away, for the wedding at 2:30. Sue answered the door.

Katie was standing inside facing the ocean. She turned, dressed in her full- length shimmering wedding gown, wearing her grandmother's veil, and looked at me. It was a father/daughter moment that made me remember her birth, her first Easter dress, her college graduation at UC Davis with the lei around her neck. Now this.

"Please, don't make me cry, Dad," she said. I didn't, and smiled instead. The tears ran inward like a waterfall.

The rehearsal is one thing, but walking your daughter down the aisle is one of the most joyous and bittersweet moments in a man's life. I would do it again tomorrow.

During the ceremony when we were asked to remember the sick and those who could not come today, I thought of Wendy Wayne. Sue and I looked at each other at the same time and teared up.

The reception started at 5:30. You've heard of James Brown? Move on over. Herb Brown, James' long lost brother, was in the building.

I danced almost every dance. I had signature moves (the most notable one I cover in a later column).

One of the best moments, among many, was seeing my parents on the floor dancing. My mom danced with Father Jerry. She's not big on religion, but she liked Father Jerry, and he was a smooth dancer.

My dad is a pro, too.

"I have about three moves anymore," he said later. "I just swap them out."

My toast looked great on paper, as many of them do, but four lines into it, I was still looking for my first laugh. I settled for a chuckle in line No. 5 and then thanked the Oliver's for raising three good men, one of whom had the good sense to marry my daughter. Then I said, "One blue eye and one brown eye. When she was born, the doctors said it was a one in 30,000 chance."

After the wedding, I was hungry. I went back to the hotel room and saw a large bag of Cheetos.

Should I dare eat a handful of Cheetos in a tux?

Sunday, we had that after-wedding glow. Monday and Tuesday, too. The elation has lasted most of the week, and not just for us.

Fred Oliver, Hunter's father, has called three times. He was doing paperwork and thought about the wedding. He can't let go either.

DAD SERVES UP SOME PUNCH AT THE RECEPTION

The last dance of the evening was "You Never Can Tell," or so we thought, until Nick Andrews, the DJ, said, "Now, we have one more song that is a favorite of the Benhams."

Then he played "Born to Run."

Katie was married last weekend to Hunter Oliver. She is now Katie Benham Oliver. Katie Oliver. Those names sound like they were born to be together.

When Katie and her three brothers were under the age of 12, our family anthem was "Born to Run." We'd put the song on after dinner and before bedtime. The song demands movement, and the kids would run around the house like little monkeys.

There is a moment in "Born to Run," about two-thirds the way through, when the E Street Band goes into a descending group of chords and then Springsteen comes back in with "One, two, three, four ... The highway's lined with broken heroes on a last-chance power drive."

During this break, I would crouch on the floor, put my head on the carpet and when Springsteen sang "One, two, three, four!" I would leap to my feet and the kids would shriek with happiness.

By the last dance at Katie and Hunter's wedding, there were about 20 guests left, including Katie, dressed in her beautiful ivory wedding gown, along with Herbie, Sam and Thomas in gray suits.

Why not? Let's return to the way it was on 20th and Cedar. Halfway through the song, I crouched on all fours on the wooden dance floor. Lauren, Sam's girlfriend, tapped me on the shoulder.

"Mr. Benham, are you OK?" she asked.

I looked up at her. She hadn't heard about my signature move. I smiled and nodded.

She tapped me on the shoulder again. She was afraid I'd gone down, felled by a heart attack or a stroke, and should she and Sam decide on something more permanent, she was concerned I might not be present to dance at their wedding.

"One, two, three, four!"

Powered by my chromium hip, I sprung up in my extra shiny black shoes and black tuxedo like it was 1994, and as I did, I thrust my fist in the air celebrating all that was good about life and holy matrimony -- and socked Katie in the face.

A lot of things go through your mind when you accidently catch your daughter with a haymaker at her wedding.

What part of her lovely face did I hit? There are hard parts of a face and soft parts. The nose is a soft part and so are the lips. If you have to sock your daughter, you're better off punching her in the jaw or forehead.

A couple of hours earlier, we had enjoyed a sweet father/daughter dance to "Tupelo Honey." Then, I had proposed a loving toast talking about my girl with one brown eye and one blue, one in 30,000.

Now, this.

I've hit people harder before. Ask Bobby Poff. I hit him so hard I'm not certain he graduated from the fourth grade. However, I haven't hit anyone else in 45 years. I am a man of peace with the occasion stormy thought, but somebody who normally can be trusted at a wedding.

Katie ran away. Who could blame her?

She was concerned about getting blood on her dress and how did she know I didn't have a left cross in my repertoire?

"Katie, are you OK?"

By this point, I'd caught up with her and she was seated in one of the dining room chairs and had her head down.

"I just don't want to have a fat lip on my wedding night," she said.

There have been times in the past when I thought she tended to overreact, but it probably wasn't too much to ask to finish your wedding night without stitches.

She dabbed at her lip with a white linen napkin. My punch had landed on her lower lip and a quick inspection revealed that her teeth were intact.

She dabbed at the inside of her mouth and there were a couple of spots of blood.

"Katie, you're going to be fine," Hunter said, giving her the once-over. "I've been hit harder in soccer games."

An hour later, after we had left the club, I texted her and asked her how she was doing.

"I'm great. It's not a problem. I'm going to be fine."

Good, because baby, you were born to run.

WENDY WAYNE

One of the things I will remember about Wendy Wayne: after whatever modest greeting I gave her, she'd pause, take the floor, and look me straight in the eye with that Wendy twinkle and say, "How are you doing?"

Emphasis was on the "you." Wendy said "you" as if "you" were the only "you" in the world and as if she couldn't wait to hear what jewels would fall out your mouth.

Wendy Wayne inspired people, sometimes in different ways. Wendy fed the poor, administered to the sick, built latrines in Africa, and opened her home to every orphan between here and New York. I found myself giving a dollar to the homeless, picking up plastic cup lids and being less curt to the old and the miserable, trying to measure up.

However, Wendy was so good, so unselfish and so consistent in her beliefs, it became overwhelming. I couldn't get up that early or stay up that late. It was just as easy to say, "Well, Wendy has that covered." Or, on the heels of another disaster in a Third World country, "Wendy will volunteer."

In other words, I felt like I was a better person just knowing her. The way I looked at it was, you could add her contribution to your contribution and divide by two, and the "make the world a better place" average was still high.

A few weeks ago, Wendy sent me a birthday card. I'm not trying to sound special because I suspect Wendy bought her greeting cards by the bushel and sent them to scores of people.

"2012
Herb —
Sending warm wishes from down the street to our longtime friend & neighbor. May this year (besides bringing a new addition to the family) bring you many dreams realized.

Fondly,
Wendy and Gene."

This was vintage Wendy in two ways: First of all giving Gene co-credit. I like Gene — Gene's a friend, but I'm telling you Gene didn't write that card. Not only did Wendy take the time to send warm wishes, but she did it when she was undoubtedly feeling lousy.

That's Wendy. Another example of "How are you doing?"

When she became sick four years ago and started her treatments, I saw her one day and asked if she wanted to take a walk. I couldn't help with the chemo, radiation and stem cell transplant, but we could walk. I was hoping that we could walk the cancer right out of her body.

Wendy went into remission and started feeling better. Almost every time I saw her for the next two years, she'd refer to the time we walked together. It was as if I had done something worthy of being nominated for the Nobel Peace Prize.

I probably had company. Wendy nominated a lot of people, and we all felt like winners.

When the rains came that winter, followed by fog and sunshine, I asked her if she wanted to go mushroom hunting near Calloway, north of the river. She did and for a first-timer she was a good mushroom hunter. By the turnaround point, close to the stand of old cottonwood trees, Wendy was spotting villages of mushrooms and bounding after them like a little girl with her mass of black curls bouncing, now grown back after the chemo.

She was happy and couldn't wait to go again.

It rained a lot that winter, enough so that water flowed bank to bank in the river. During the summer, we launched paddleboards from Beach Park and paddled down to River Walk. It was like the great snow, probably a once-in-a-lifetime occurrence, and we couldn't get enough.

Wendy heard about it and asked if she could go. She was game, supremely game. Game like my mother is game.

Finally, toward the end of the season with the water only 2 feet deep now, we pushed off, starting at Beach and floating underneath the 99 bridge, past Yokuts, the par course, portaging at the dirt plug near Coffee, going back in the water, and leaving the river at the parking lot at California Pizza Kitchen where Gene was parked.

I will remember Wendy in that last section because the river was peaceful, wide, and the sun was going down. There was this lovely golden light in her face. She was beaming. With Wendy you were never sure. Was that the sun reflecting off her face or was Wendy reflecting off the sun?

When we told our four children that Wendy was sick, had refused all future treatment and was now home with her family, our son Herbie wrote a letter, which is excerpted below:

Dear Wendy,

When I reflect on my upbringing in Bakersfield, it seems magical and the stuff of legend. Growing up downtown, going to Franklin and BHS, work parties and the best Halloween and Fourth of July parties. Larkin, Benji and Dominic were my first heroes, guys I looked up to more than anything who were great teachers and big brothers.

Of all the adults that I was around as a kid, it was you who made me feel more comfortable in my own skin than anyone. I know you extend your hospitality to everyone equally, but being over at your house was to receive the royal treatment. Not only were you always showering us with chocolate chip cookies, pretzels or whatever delicious home-cooked food you had around, but you had a way of listening that was unmatched. I know that's because you genuinely cared, but when I talked to you I felt like a person, not a kid. Your house was just the most lively, comforting place to be, because of the vibe of love you so effortlessly cultivated.

Conversations with you have always been real and seamless because you might be the least judgmental person I have ever met. Throughout my darker teenage years and early 20s, it was always easy to be around you when I felt somewhat contemptuous of other adults and authority figures. Books could be, and should be, written on your contributions to humanity at large, but I feel like I hit the lottery in life just knowing you as a friend.

A couple months ago, before a bartending shift in downtown SF, I was thinking about you and decided to buy about 20 Subway sandwiches and give them to the homeless people that live in the alley behind the restaurant. On this particular day I was feeling sorry for myself for whatever stupid reason, and I thought about you and what you have been going through and decided I needed to throw some good energy into the world. You have always been the Queen of Good Energy.

Thank you for being my friend, Wendy. For your patience, your warmth, your unconditional kindness. My life is richer knowing you. I love you and am inspired by you forever.

Love

Herbie Benham IV

The letter reminded me of one of Wendy's greatest strengths. She loved your children almost more than you did. She loved them when they were unlovable. She saw through the teenage years like Superman could see through brick walls.

Once you were in, you were in, and for Wendy, kids were in. She received an enormous kick from young people and there are probably hundreds who will honor her memory by trying to be like her.

What are we going to do now? We can no longer add her contributions to ours and divide by two. If she could, she would be rooting for "you" to make the world a better place.

We were slotted in to visit Wendy at 4 p.m. Sunday. When we heard the news she had died that morning, we were told that Gene would welcome company.

He told us it was typical Wendy near the end. When Gene and family friends went into the other room to watch the Dodger game on Saturday, she came in and lay on the leather couch that she loved so she could be with everyone.

That night, she slept on the couch and Gene slept in the comfort of the hospital bed. She would have wanted it no other way.

CALLIE COMES HOME

Every cat has endearing qualities, and Callie was no different. She had a trick. She'd roll over on her side on the front sidewalk when someone approached — friend or stranger — as if to invite them to stroke her soft, silky fur.

I understand. Everybody has the best cat in the world. We had Callie.

Callie was 18. Even so, I kept hoping for miracles. Maybe there was a 10th life out there.

Blind? We specialize in blind pets. When Callie's eyes clouded over a year or so ago, she fit right in with Poco, our blind chocolate lab.

Sleep more and more? That's what cats do. They make their living being relaxed and rubbing against your neck when you are sitting on the sofa.

Cats have the life we wish we had. The day they come to live with us, they are retired, with periodic side jobs that do not affect their unemployment benefits.

"We have to talk about Callie," Sue said a few weeks ago.

I knew what was coming, but I was like the seven other runners in the 100-meter race in the Olympics. I was hoping for a miracle that precluded a 6-foot-5 Jamaican.

"I've been cleaning up underneath the dining room table lately,' she said.

I'd seen that and hoped it wasn't what I had thought it was. Maybe a pipe had burst. The ceiling had leaked.

"We have to be compassionate," she said. Sue was no Lizzie Borden swinging an ax. When our friend Bob Smith showed up at our door 18 years ago with Callie in his bike jersey, having found this bedraggled kitten in the Elks Lodge flowerbed, Sue had protested at first.

"I have four small children," she said. "Why do I need a kitten, too?"

Turns out she did, and over the next 18 years when the children were being good, bad and indifferent, Callie slept on her pillow, greeted her on the sidewalk when she came home, and sat on her lap while she did crossword puzzles.

Sue was Callie's favorite, and her only competition was Thomas, whose bed Callie slept on until he left for college.

"Let her settle in," he'd instruct one or more of his siblings when they visited, as if he were giving them parenting advice. "Don't be too anxious to pet her."

Then, Thomas left, and Callie went from a cat to the third person in the room to whom we would direct conversation.

We should have seen it coming, but I have found denial to be an effective coping strategy. Callie stopped sleeping with us recently. She stopped making the regular trek up to our room when we were getting ready for bed.

Callie declined to go outside, her meow became more plaintive, like a boat in distress approaching a harbor on a foggy night.

If it were possible, Callie slept even more than she had before, breaking the previous world record of 22 hours a day.

A couple of days ago, her tail, with a white spot at the tip, stopped moving like a baton. The conductor was bringing the symphony to a graceful close.

Callie was winding down. It made me think of something my dad once said: "It takes time to go broke." Callie was giving us plenty of opportunities to say goodbye.

"I think we should do something," Sue said. "She is suffering."

It's not easy to make that call. The vet's number was busy when I first dialed. A sign, I thought. Five minutes later, the call went through.

I drove slowly. Sue had Callie on her lap wrapped in a pink towel and, for once, Callie didn't meow in the car or turn her head. I know I'm reading too much into this, but it was as if she knew where she was going and wanted us to know that she had accepted it.

"I'm OK," I imagined her saying. "Don't be sad for me. We've had fun."

Like I said, it's easy to go off the ledge when you have a great cat.

"Give her a kiss for me," Sam texted his mother.

My God. Could this be any harder? I half expected to pull up at the vet's and have the flag flying at half-staff.

"Have you called Thomas?" I asked when we pulled into the parking lot.

She had and left a message, barely making it through the call.

There is a song I've been listening to lately by Woody Guthrie that uses the word touchstone. A good cat is like a touchstone. She makes everybody feel more serene.

I buried her on the side of the house by the woodpile. She's close to Polo, the homely pit bull mix with the weak heart and sweet soul. Both strays who were initially unwanted and ultimately loved, they belong together.

Life is wonderful, but for it to be wonderful it has to have balance. That means it can hurt, but for a few bags of cat food, it's worth it.

Like millions before her, Callie was a bargain.

Thanks, Bob, even though Sue was mad at you at the time.

Thank you, Callie June. I will think of you reclining on every soft surface in the house. Think of you when I pull up, look at the sidewalk and remember how relaxed you were.

Welcome home, Callie. Welcome home.

A PROPOSAL THAT PLEASES ALL IN FAMILY

He proposed to her on top of the highest hill in Norwich, England, as the sun was setting. Who knew? Who knew Sam had a romantic streak?

"Sam, how do you know she is going to say yes?" his younger brother, Thomas, asked prior to Sam buying the ring, boarding the plane and taking the train.

"I'm giving her a 30 percent chance of coming to her senses and saying no."

That's a brother for you. That's what brothers do. They provide clarity and a vote of confidence.

She said yes. God knows why she said yes, but she did.

What a long strange trip it's been.

The Grateful Dead lyric is worn, but fits. Especially with children. You start in one place, move to another and end up in a third. Sunshine, rain, fog, howling winds, you get it all. It's like the first scene in "The Wizard of Oz." One minute there is a tornado and the next, you're dancing with the Munchkins.

Then, one day, this:

"Dad, I think I'm going to propose to Lauren," Sam said a few weeks ago.

We were sitting in his house. His mother had already gone home. It was late, but never too late for this kind of conversation.

The room had been quiet before. It got quieter. You could hear the sprinklers click on outside. Crickets.

I think I said something. The announcement called for a response but other than telling him I thought it was a good idea, I didn't say much.

There are talking times and listening times. This was a listening time, and Sam was somebody who was past advice or commentary.

Four years together. That's sufficient. If you don't know each other yet, it may be that you're watching too much "SportsCenter."

I'll say this: He's lucky. She's straightforward, kind and sunny. She even wanted to invite Sam's grandparents to their Fourth of July party when Sam's grandparents were old enough to be ... Sam's grandparents.

If I'm going to use the most quoted line in the Grateful Dead catalog, I might as well dovetail into Tom Cruise and Renee Zellweger in "Jerry Maguire" when he tells her, "You complete me." Lauren completes Sam.

"Lauren is the sweetest person I've ever met," Sam said awhile back.

Game, set and match. If this one doesn't work, we should be worried about marriage. Maybe return to living in treehouses and dating between hunts.

"Sam, you tell your mother," I said that night. "That's your news to tell."

Sam did, two weeks later. He drove 200 miles from Bakersfield to Del Mar (there was the beach waiting, too) to tell her.

I've seen her happy: births of her four children, a ticket to Paris, being 20 rows from Bruce Springsteen, but this was up there.

Her tears almost set Sam off and he's not that kind of guy. That's Lauren and the "you complete me" part.

"We have to call Nancy and Alan," Sue said. "Fred and Susan called us when Hunter and Katie decided to get married. Emily Post says it's up to the groom's parents to place that call."

We did. Sue first. Sue and Nancy were enthusiastic on the phone. There's nothing women like more than the prospect of a wedding, unless it's the birth of the royal baby.

Leave it to men to throw a wet blanket on it. Men do for gloom what Johnny Appleseed did for apples.

It didn't take long after Sue handed me the phone for me to start talking about the weather. It wasn't just my lack of depth. Nancy lives in Seattle. Weather is a big deal in Seattle, especially this run of clear days they're having.

Alan and I traded messages. It was sort of a verbal high five.

That's enough for guys. We'll catch up down the line with our suits on and bounce off each other with a bro hug.

Finally, a line from "Almost Famous: "It's all happening." Happening just like everybody said it would. Babies, toddlers, children, teenagers, grownups. Careers, girlfriends, boyfriends and sometimes marriage.

Good news. It completes us.

EPILOGUE

In the end, the beginning too, feature columnists depend on readers for making writing a conversation. I write for your pleasure and I hope you read for the same reason.

Thanks for indulging me over the 25 years I've worked for the paper.

I've learned this much. Our lives are similar. Joy, sorrow and laughter knit us together. It is more fun and less lonely that way.

Sue and our children — Katie, Herbie, Sam and Thomas — have been good sports. They've given me material, made me laugh, cry and reflect.

I am also grateful to other people in my life who have inspired columns. These include Oilfield Russ, Plumbing Jim, Cabinet Curt, Shafter Dolly, Cousin Bea, the Bakers, Brandons, Hills, and more recently Hunter and Lauren, new additions to our family.

Not to be forgotten are those people who have let me into their lives in moments of great sadness and joy. Thank you.

Katie, 31, is married, works for Prudential and lives in La Jolla with her husband, Hunter. Her new name is Katie Oliver, which has a nice ring to it. They gaze at palm trees, red-tiled roofs, and the Pacific Ocean. They are happy. I hope so. She is still my favorite Katie.

Sam, 27, miraculously, moved back to Bakersfield in August of 2012. We never thought one of our children would return, and if one did, we'd have bet that it would not be Sam, our most spirited child. He works in sales for Lightspeed, recently bought a house two blocks down the street from us and is engaged to Lauren.

Herbie, 29, lives in North Oakland and is actively recording and composing music. He works at the Ramen Shop in Oakland as a bartender. He is soulful and a terrific writer, better than his father, I think.

Thomas is 23, lives in Berkeley, and works as a line cook at Chez Panisse. He loves life. His mother took him to the restaurant for the first time when he was 10 and she should be held responsible for Thomas making a career in food. Her excellent cooking didn't hurt either.

Sue, the VP for Philanthropy at Bakersfield Memorial Hospital, retired from the City Council after 12 years of service. We never knew there were so many barking dogs, traffic problems, and crazy neighbors. This is to say that Sue doesn't miss the evening phone calls that provided this window on the world.

I'm proud of her steadiness and unflappability in the face of several harrowing votes, when she was the lone yay or nay, and the dignity with which she carried herself. I think some of her city council groupies miss her too.

At first I was a mess when the children left, Thomas being the last one to do so. Sue was better; she missed them in a quieter way.

Then, after a month, I enjoyed the freedom and the flexibility. We don't wait for them to come in at night, to call when they don't; there are no messages from the high school, "Your junior student missed one or more classes on Thursday."

There is satisfaction in knowing you gave a thousand percent as a parent, even if half the things you did (that I did — Sue was a much better natural parent) were wrong. If we were to raise kids again, I wouldn't sweat as much of the small stuff as I did.

Life is rich. My friends and I have a regular men's night. I joined the Bakersfield Master Chorale, and along with a group of music lovers, formed Passing Through Productions in order to bring concerts to town.

Sue and I also travel. The best part about traveling is meeting people. Good people. Just like the ones we've found here in Bakersfield.